The Wit and Wisdom of Boris Johnson

The Wit and Wisdom of Boris Johnson

Introduced and Edited by

HARRY MOUNT

B L O O M S B U R Y

LONDON • NEW DELHI • NEW YORK • SYDNEY

First published in Great Britain 2013

Copyright © Harry Mount, 2013
Preface © Charles FitzRoy, 2013

Extracts and quotations © *Daily Telegraph; Sunday Telegraph; The Spectator; Life in the Fast Lane* (Boris Johnson, Harper Perennial, 2007); *Johnson's Life of London* (Boris Johnson, HarperPress, 2011); *The Rise of Boris Johnson* (Andrew Gimson, Simon and Schuster, 2012); *The Oxford Myth* (ed. Rachel Johnson, Weidenfeld & Nicolson, 1998)

A Continuum book

Bloomsbury Publishing Plc
50 Bedford Square
London WC1B 3DP

www.bloomsbury.com

Bloomsbury Publishing, London, New Delhi, New York and Sydney

A CIP record for this book is available from the British Library.

ISBN 9781408183526

10 9 8 7 6 5 4 3 2 1

Typeset by Fakenham Prepress Solutions, Fakenham, Norfolk NR21 8NN
Printed and bound in Great Britain by CPI Group (UK) Ltd, Croydon, CR0 4YY

CONTENTS

PREFACE

It was down in the crypt of St Paul's Cathedral that I first discovered that Boris was my cousin. We were there to celebrate the centenary of a mutual ancestor, Sir George Williams. It seems somewhat unlikely we should both be descended from this largely forgotten Victorian figure, founder of the YMCA, once the largest young man's Christian organisation in the world. Boris's father Stanley gave an excellent, impromptu speech, drawing threads between all the various members of the extended family, most of whom had no idea they were related, so that, by the end of the evening, we all felt pleased to be kinsmen. Ever since, whenever we meet, we greet each other as cousins, although the words 'Cousin Boris' give a Russian flavour, as if set in a novel by Turgenev. My sons love the idea that they are related to the great man, particularly my son George, with his mop of blond hair, who has been nick-named Boris at school, and bathes in his reflected glory.

It was shortly after the service in St Paul's that I had the idea of inviting Boris to Rome to lecture for my company Fine Art Travel. By great good fortune, this was shortly before he stood to be Mayor of London, and hit superstardom. A weekend in Rome was the perfect opportunity to get to know him and his charming wife Marina. It was also the chance to witness first-hand the Boris phenomenon. At its simplest, this is a mixture of originality, humour and charisma. What is so interesting is how prominent these attributes were on a tour of ancient Rome, not, you might think, the most obvious place to display them.

We started off the tour in the Capitoline Museums, where we were treated to a short display of Boris the politician, telling us about the Treaty of Rome, which was signed here. The forming of the European Economic Community was a key event in 20th century European history but the institution's failings has made it an easy target for any eurosceptic Conservative politician worth his salt, and Boris was soon weighing in. Enjoyable as this was, however, we were all much keener to hear what the great man had to say about the ancient Romans, and so I urged him to lead us into the museum of sculpture (characteristically, I noticed that he had left behind the catalogue I had sent him and so had, almost certainly, failed to mug it up).

I should not have worried. Admirers of Boris will know that the expression 'ad lib' could have been designed specifically for him. Certainly, any budding art historian, brought up to regard the Capitoline Museum's array of classical sculpture as the summit of excellence, would have been somewhat surprised at his method of lecturing. Stopping in front of the *Dying Gaul,* one of the most famous of all classical statues, whose nobility and pathos has inspired Byron and many others, Boris proceeded to take a highly original line. His theme was the role of trousers in the ancient world, and how they were only worn by losers. If you were a winner, you most certainly wore a toga, but the *Dying Gaul,* bleeding to death in the Colosseum, was definitely a loser (such was the power of our *professore's* argument that nobody seemed to notice that the Gaul is not, in fact, wearing trousers at all). Just to add a dash of humour he made a further disparaging remark about the statue, referring to his mullet-headed haircut.

Boris displayed the same light touch when confronted by the Pantheon. It is one of the city's great charms that such a magnificent building should be tucked away in a surprisingly small piazza. After a convivial lunch, we rounded the corner and there Hadrian's masterpiece stood before us in all its glory. It was too good a moment to miss so I asked Boris to tell us about the building. Without a moment's hesitation, he pointed at the pediment and said: 'You see that inscription – it says *M. Agrippa fecit*. Well, the Pantheon was built by the Emperor Hadrian, you all know him from the Wall in England put up to keep out those barbaric Scots. But before Hadrian there was another Pantheon on this site, erected by Marcus Agrippa, as you can see on the pediment. He was the right-hand man of the Emperor Augustus and, whenever Augustus was in a bit of trouble, he would say 'Get Agrippa'.

This was, of course, exactly what we had come to hear: information imparted with wit, though it was clear that a couple of Americans in the group were rather perplexed by these words of wisdom. They were still more bemused when a number of British passers-by stopped to greet our lecturer with the words: 'Hi, Boris, what are you doing here; are you running in the marathon?', an event that was taking place in Rome the next day.

There is, of course, a mercurial element to Boris Johnson, and this is one of his main attractions to those who relish his unpredictability. A friend told me of a major charitable event he helped to organise. At the gala dinner, Boris was the guest speaker. The dinner started at 8 p.m. and, by 8.30, there was still no sign of the great man. Suddenly he appeared, looking, in my friend's words, 'as if he had been through a hedge backwards'. Rather flustered, he sat down and proceeded to ask a series of rapid-fire questions about the event, noting down his answers on the napkin, and ignoring his food. At the end of the meal he rose to his feet and delivered a speech that bore almost no relation to all the information he had just been given. This rather annoyed my friend, but what he found even more galling was that the audience loved it, and left for home, quoting the great man's *bons mots* and still laughing at his jokes.

It was while recounting these and other tales of Boris in the office that the idea of this book first emerged. I am quite sure that it will be a great source of enjoyment.

Lord Charles FitzRoy
April 2013

INTRODUCTION

One evening, towards the end of 2012, I thanked Boris Johnson for letting me edit this book. The conversation that followed goes a little way to unpeeling the planet-brained, blond onion that is his character.

It was at the launch, in a Tower Bridge pub, of his sister Rachel's novel, *Winter Games*, about upper-class English girls in Nazi Germany before the war. Rachel – no slouch in the PR department – was in lederhosen and had laid on an 'oompah' band and plates of bratwurst to get us in the Teutonic mood. Her speech – on how to give a launch party – lampooned the limp party-planning advice of her fellow Penguin author, Pippa Middleton – "First, you'll definitely need some drink..."

And then Boris arrived – late, as usual, but genuinely trying to be as surreptitious as possible. He didn't stand a chance. Like Elvis turning up at his kid sister's party, he was mobbed on all sides by friends, relations and complete strangers. In a bid to deflect attention, he tried to make himself useful – he made for the bar and proceeded to send a convoy of glasses of red wine over the heads of the throng to his wife, Marina, and various other members of the Johnson clan. The *I'm-just-here-to-help* ploy didn't work. The crowd of acolytes circled closer, pressing him up against the bar.

It's hard to overstate not just Boris's fame, but also the affection he's held in. A lot of the reason for the affection is the well-practised, mock-bumbling, Latin-loving routine – Billy Bunter meets Bertie Wooster meets Professor Brainstorm. But he is also very unlike most politicians – often a humourless, didactic, upwardly managing group – in that he is extremely adept at spreading the love, in all directions.

At another recent book party – yup, another Johnson, his father, Stanley, was launching a collection of his journalism at the Marylebone branch of Daunt Books – Boris was besieged by customers who happened to be in the bookshop at the time. One pensioner wanted her photo taken with him; another berated him about the Tory policy on Europe. A friend of mine, a lady in her late 70s, went up to him and said, "I think you're much better than David Cameron, and should really be in charge."

"My devotion to the dear leader is absolute," said Boris, with such intense mock seriousness that you couldn't help but think the opposite. He threw in a batsqueak of flirtatiousness, too. With a gleam in her eyes, my friend confessed to me afterwards that she had been utterly bewitched by him.

With none of the crowd, at either party, did he show the slightest flicker of irritation, or any of the code words that suggest you want to end a conversation – "Well, it's been lovely to meet you," that sort of thing. He naturally inhabits the hallowed, clichéd persona of the ideal politician – he remembers you, and he makes you think that he really likes you.

At his sister's party, I couldn't get close enough to thank him for letting me do this book, but he singled me out with a thrusting index finger.

"Harry!" he boomed, as if we were bosom childhood companions who hadn't seen each other for decades – rather than friendly old work colleagues (I used to work on the *Daily Telegraph* with him for five years) who bump into each other quite a lot.

I went on to thank him. He professed to have no idea at all about the existence of this book – even though he had given it the go-ahead the week before. Despite his prodigious memory, there is a small chance he might have forgotten all about it. Although lots of Boris's friends say he's lazy, the volume of work he deals with, as mayor and journalist, is colossal. On Wednesday evenings in the early 2000s – when I used to edit his *Telegraph* column – he also wrote the leader for the *Spectator*, went to Prime Minister's Questions (PMQs) and wrote a car column for *GQ* magazine.

Then again, the chances are, he probably did know all about the book. Part of the Boris mystique is to veil all sorts of things in a miasma of faux ignorance – it flatters the person he's talking to, who then comes across as knowing more. When he was appointed shadow Arts Minister on 7 May 2004, his response was, "Look the point is... er, what is the point? It is a tough job but somebody has got to do it."

Daniel Hannan, the Conservative MEP, says of Boris's pretend stupidity, "It's a great rhetorical trick to say, 'I've got five policies, erm, what are they?'"

"He's brilliantly worked out that English people don't like clever intellectuals, particularly in the Conservative audience he wants to appeal to. There's a smooth machine under the buffoonery. It's not an exaggeration to call him a genius."

The faux ignorance technique also doubles as a perverse device for advertising his intellect. An MP friend of mine describes a three-way conversation he once had with Boris and a conservation expert. The MP was discussing the best way to save the African elephant.

"The thing you've got to do is sell off the land to private investors," said the MP.

"Christ, that seems awfully odd," said Boris.

"Well, if the state owns the land, then the wardens just poach the elephants for themselves," said the MP, "but if you privatise the land, and reward the wardens for increasing tourist numbers, then they have an interest in the elephants surviving."

The conservation expert turned out to be rather impressed by the MP's line. Noticing the transfer of the limelight, Boris quickly shifted gear from clueless ingénue to African elephant expert.

"Ah, yes! It's coming back to me – the McTavish report, isn't it? Now of course it's worked much better with Tanzanian elephants than Zimbabwean ones..."

The faux ignorance ploy has other benefits, too. Because the public have – front of mind – the idea of Boris as a bumbling fool, they let him get away with high-brow references. In his 2012 Tory Conference speech, Boris talked of the "eupepsia, euphoria, eudaimonia" brought on by the Olympics. No other politician could use words like that, without coming across as too dangerously clever by half.

His *That's-News-To-Me-Guv* approach also

helps get him off the hook. He used the technique many times during the years I edited his *Telegraph* column. Week after week, my Wednesday nights were destroyed by Boris filing so late. His *Telegraph* column was the last thing he did – long after the *Spectator* had been put to bed, PMQs was over, and the *GQ* car column had been filed.

All the other regular columnists on the *Telegraph* had to file by 4 p.m., and they kept rigorously to their deadlines. Boris was given special dispensation; again and again in his professional, and his private life, he has been given special dispensation by friends, family and frustrated colleagues who can't help but like him. As his biographer, Andrew Gimson, told me, "He's like the boy in the nativity play who's forgotten his lines who you're longing to help out."

So Boris was allowed to file by 7 p.m.; but, still, week after week, he was late.

On the dot of 7 p.m., I – and, over the years, many other colleagues on the *Telegraph* Comment desk – would ring his mobile. The old, hyper-friendly voice boomed over the phone.

"Should be with you now, boss," said Boris, who can lay on flattery with a supersized trowel. It's ridiculous when he introduces me at parties as his old editor. His prose never needed an editor – just a poor chimp prepared to check his emails late into the night on Wednesday evenings and send Boris's word-perfect, pitch-perfect copy on to the subs. But the head still swells a bit when the great man apparently defers to you, even though you know, in his heart, he defers to no one.

It helps that Boris has an exceptional memory for the times he's met you before. On the evening of his fringe speech at the 2012 Tory Conference, both Anne Diamond and the journalist Vincent Graff told stories of how Boris remembered precise details of brief conversations they'd had with him years ago.

Bill Clinton did the same, filing people's names and details in a Rolodex, and remembering them many years later. Boris manages without the Rolodex and those who come across him – and work for him – reward his prodigious memory with affection.

A builder who once put up an extension in Islington for the Johnsons told a friend of mine he's so keen on Boris that he took time off work to vote for him. A Conservative adviser who has worked with him on many campaigns told me that, uniquely among senior Tories, Boris always chats to him, remembers his name and leaves him with a sort of Ready-Brek glow.

If you talk to Boris at a party, he never scans the place for the great and the good – he's too confident to feel he must work a room. In any case, he doesn't have to make the effort: the mountain may not come to Mohammed, but the great and the good make their way to Boris.

It helps, too, that his first name is so memorable, rare and comic, that everyone tends to refer to him by it, immediately assuming a familiarity and friendliness. When Barclays sponsored the London cycle hire scheme in 2010, they might have reasonably hoped they would be called Barclays Bikes – they didn't stand a chance up against the Boris branding.

Anyway, back to my destroyed Wednesday evenings.

"It hasn't arrived," I'd say at 7.01 p.m..

"Ah, Christ, sorry," said Boris who – again, unlike most politicians – is extremely good at apologising. He long ago learnt the ancient English art of saying sorry without meaning it. "Bloody internet! It must be pinging its way down those threadbare copper wires, as we speak, old man."

It wasn't doing anything of the sort, because Boris had yet to put pen to paper; sometimes you could hear him bashing away at his keyboard in the background, just as he was telling you he'd sent it ages ago.

His technical incompetence was real enough. He once asked the chief sub on the *Telegraph* Comment desk to translate a piece he'd typed with the shift key accidentally deployed, back into lower case. An article that read

203498BARROSO230"!INTERGALACTIC
&NUMBSKULL%2#_ turned out in fact to be
a learned piece on the case against the euro. It
showed, too, the lightning speed he can write at
when he's under the cosh – typing away without
a glance at the screen.

Excuses like this poured out of the phone
every week and, every week, the editor or
deputy editor of the Comment pages had their
Wednesday night ruined. Charles Moore, his
old *Telegraph* editor, got Boris right when he
borrowed the words used by David Niven of
Errol Flynn, "You knew where you were with
Errol Flynn. He always let you down."

It's true, and it's truer the closer you get to
Boris. The fans, like the elderly lady at the party,
get the charm and the stardust sprinkled in their
gleaming eyes. The people working for, or with,
him get the charm, too, but they also have to
toil to fill the gap left by his over-extended
commitments, his ambition and the Olympian
confidence that so often leaves him unprepared.

Ian Hislop has said that most guest chairmen
of *Have I Got News For You?* rehearse the script
for two days; Boris used to arrive at 6 p.m., as
recording began, and let his lack of preparation
produce its own form of comedy.

But the thing is, however many of my
Wednesday night drinks and dinners were
destroyed by Boris, it was impossible to dislike

him, not least because of his strange generosity of heart. When his two biographers – Andrew Gimson and Sonia Purnell – approached me for Boris anecdotes for their books, I boringly stonewalled them; for all those miserable Wednesday evenings, it felt like treachery to tell on him – as I am doing now.

It would have seemed disloyal, in a way that Boris rarely is. He'll let you down but he won't tell tales on you. Boris is again rare among politicians, in that it's very difficult to get him to be rude about his colleagues; rare among people, too, in possessing the ability to be funny without resorting to the easy weapons of rudeness and gossip.

For someone who is so keen on becoming a very important person, he is remarkably free from self-importance. A few years ago, I sent him a copy of a book on Latin I was writing, hoping for a quote for the cover. More pompous, less self-confident public figures often refuse to do this sort of thing on principle, for fear of diluting their brand, of giving praise that really should only be allotted to them.

Boris said that, to be honest, he didn't have time to read my book, but proceeded to give me several quotes, adding, "Or just make one up, if you want." The one I chose – "Learn Latin – the only way forwards is backwards!" was characteristically pithy and well-calibrated.

For all his gaffes – his insults to Liverpool, Portsmouth and Papua New Guinea, the affairs – Boris is in fact a brilliant calibrator. He knows exactly how much he can get away with, when not to take the blame, when to take it. When people try to attack him – like the BBC's Eddie Mair, who called him "a nasty piece of work" in March 2013 – the criticism just slides off the poor little boy who's forgotten his lines.

Not everyone falls for his laser beam charm. A sizeable proportion of the newspaper commentariat dislike Boris; MPs, too. Much of this is down to jealousy – at Boris riding both the political and journalistic horses so well, and being so handsomely rewarded for it, too.

MPs in particular took against him when he edited the *Spectator*. They were amazed that Boris didn't publish their mind-numbingly dull pieces on 'Whither the euro?' It's surprising how many politicians don't really understand the mechanics of a magazine – the editor commissions pieces; he doesn't passively receive them from anyone with a shopworn opinion to sell.

Their criticisms have little effect; ditto the gaffes. Boris's gaffe trajectory is the opposite of that old cliché – it's not the crime that gets you; it's the cover-up. Boris gets off scot-free from both the crime and the cover-up, because of his magical gift for surreal, amusing apology. It works like a sort of bulletproof armour – political and personal scandals that would sink other politicians just rebound off him into the long grass, where they're quickly forgotten.

He didn't in fact write the *Spectator* leader attacking Liverpudlians but, still, he went up to Liverpool to apologise. Since then, he has, at his own admission, made something of a speciality of gifted apologies.

In 2006, he said of the Tory Party that it had "become used to Papua New Guinea-style orgies of cannibalism and chief-killing". Shortly afterwards, he said, "I mean no insult to the people of Papua New Guinea who I'm sure lead lives of blameless bourgeois domesticity in common with the rest of us. Add Papua New Guinea to my global itinerary of apologies."

Much of the intention of Johnsonian wit and wisdom is that crucial Johnsonian mission – to get him off the hook. When he denied his affair with Petronella Wyatt, he called it "an inverted pyramid of piffle". The affair did take place but it has been largely forgotten by the public – it certainly hasn't harmed his career the way it would that of most other politicians – while the funniness and inventiveness of the quotation is remembered. Once more, he slides off that hook, not surreptitiously, but in plain view of a packed house, laughing in the aisles.

"Piffle" is a typical Johnson word; like so many of his words, it is Wodehousian – and Billy

Bunteresque – in its consciously old-fashioned, stagey, mock-posh way. He used it in an early article defending private schools, written in the *Eton Chronicle* on December 12th, 1980, when he was 16:

"I tell you this. The Civilised World can ignore, must ignore entirely, these idiots who tell us that, by their very existence, the public schools demolish all hopes most cherished for the Comprehensive System. Clearly, this is twaddle, utter bunkum, balderdash, tommyrot, piffle and fiddlesticks of the most insidious kind. So strain every nerve, parents of Britain, to send your son to this educational establishment (forget the socialist gibberish about the destruction of the state system). Exercise your freedom of choice because, in this way, you will imbue your son with the most important thing, a sense of his own importance."

Boris learnt early on the power of high-falutin words and overstated, jolly-good-chap Englishness – his school and university contemporaries tell me that the 21st century Boris character is just a grown-up version of the young Boris character in short trousers.

The funny thing is, though, Boris isn't really very English. I don't mean by blood. Although it's true that his eighth of Turkish blood – and his middle-class origins – give him an outsider-among-insiders edge in modern, blue-blooded Conservative politics. He can lampoon the poshness that David Cameron – the pure British, upper-middle-class one – does so much to play down.

By exaggerating the poshness, Boris diminishes its importance. I once saw him at a party on the same day a newspaper printed a photograph of George Osborne in the Bullingdon Club. To my eternal shame, I was standing in the picture next to him. In the middle of the crowded party, Boris approached me, bellowing, "Buller, Buller, Buller!"

I – who had done my utmost to keep my membership quiet – had been ashamed of it for years. Boris, who'd shouted it from the rooftops, hadn't given it a second thought, and, as a result, it had had no impact at all on his electoral successes. That lack of shame is very un-English, not least when it comes to his affairs – where Boris behaves much more like a French politician.

The super-posh English persona is just one of the arrows Boris pulls out of his quiver to suit the circumstances. As this collection of his words shows, Boris is a protean figure, a shape-shifter or, as one of his *Telegraph* colleagues called him, a greased albino piglet – the sort of animal you find in a booth at the Alabama State Fair; $50 if you catch the pig and hold on to him.

You never can catch Boris – he's too heavily greased up with intelligence and humour. Make someone laugh and it's hard for them to stay angry with you. And it is striking how, as well as saying funny things, he just is funny. It's not just the shambolic hair, or its bright colour. He has funny bones that appeal to people who are normally completely uninterested in politics.

Stephen Robinson, a former Comment Editor of the *Telegraph*, says of him, "He is blessed with what might be called a presumption of hilarity. Maybe it's the shock of straw-coloured hair or the extravagant hand gestures, or the way he puckers his lips before he talks, but people expect what he says to be funny, or mischievous, or indiscreet, so they may even be laughing before he has opened his mouth."

A teenage girl – who I used to teach Latin – has lined her room with pictures of him, despite being of impeccable Left-wing credentials. She just finds him innately funny.

And the same is true of most people. I play a little game with myself whenever I see a picture of Boris in the papers: I look to see whether the people around him are laughing or not. There is always at least one person who is, whether it's the doomed Conservative candidate, Maria Hutchings, on the stump with him in February 2013 in the Eastleigh by-election; or London schoolchildren being taught by Boris about the Olympic flame in 2012.

On each of these occasions, Boris is, like the best stand-up comedians, always getting the measure of the crowd – calibrating, calibrating – to pitch his act at the right level.

In 2010, I sat in on Boris Johnson giving a Latin lesson in a comprehensive school, St Saviour's and St Olave's, in Southwark, south London; the 15 girls he was teaching were enraptured.

He didn't just turn on the old comic, muddle-headed routine. He was also properly rigorous with the pupils, even in the brief half an hour he was there. The girls, who were 13 to 15, had only been doing Latin for less than a year, and, bright as they were, they only knew the basics. Boris refused to patronise them and insisted on teaching them the tricky passive: amor – I am loved; amaris – you are loved; amatur – he, she or it is loved, and so on.

As is so often the case with Boris, the shabby, blond funny-man act was a disguise to smuggle in something else. In this case, it was the present passive of amo; at other times, his humour successfully disguises, and advances, his ambition.

Stuart Reid, Boris's deputy editor at the *Spectator*, says one of Boris's favourite expressions is "bogus self-deprecation" – a peculiarly English art, the pride that apes humility. You might say that Boris is himself guilty of the sin but that wouldn't be quite right. His whole persona is an exercise in self-deprecation, perhaps – the crumpled clothes, the false ignorance, the Wodehousian bumbling – but it isn't bogus, really. The disguise is so ludicrous, so OTT, that the ambition and success are in plain sight, really.

One friend of Boris's describes meeting him just after Boris had met Roy Jenkins.

"I want to write an epic poem about Roy," said Boris, "It's amazing. He just wants everything – the fame, the power, the girls, the good life."

The friend didn't bother stating the obvious inference: that Boris could find those characteristics much closer to home.

Still, Boris manages to pull off the trick of being ambitious and successful, at the same time as implicitly mocking ambition and success. You end up forgiving him his ambition, and not begrudging him his success, because the whole act is so funny and endearing.

"Boris's eyes give him away," says Stuart Reid. "There is almost always the hint of a smile there, or even of a guffaw. Though he sincerely wants power – because he must win – he knows that all political ambition is absurd. He knows, too, that politics is absurd. The result is that, when he makes a political pitch, there is always an element of satire in his words and manner. That would be disastrous in most men, but in good ol' Boris it gets the punters in."

"He made one of his best – and most reckless – gags at a time when the Tories were running an advertising campaign with the trigger line, 'You paid the taxes...' Thus: 'You paid the taxes, where are the schools?'"

"Boris adapted the campaign to the needs of the voters in his constituency, Henley: 'You paid the taxes, where are the tennis courts?'"

"Boris is in the happy position of not having to take things seriously", continues Reid. "People of all social classes and most political persuasions will vote for him, precisely because he reduces everything to a joke while at the same time saying what the ordinary fellow feels about Europe, immigration, athletics, money..."

Boris has intuited the essential point about the British public's attitude to politics and political writing – they find it boring. Make it funny and they'll love you for ever. The answer then, is to smuggle in the seriousness in a funny costume, as he does over and over again in his *Telegraph* columns: smuggle in an attack on Saddam Hussein via an anecdote about the discovery of Tariq Aziz's cigar case; smuggle in a defence of the free market through your passion for Dairy Milk chocolate.

What Boris shows in the passages that follow is the extremely broad range of registers in the English language that he can pick and choose from. My father, Ferdinand Mount, who was the head of Margaret Thatcher's Policy Unit from 1982–3, said in his memoir, Cold Cream [2008], quite how limited her registers were. He described his time working for her as "a holiday from irony":

"It was well-known that she was resistant to humour, often had to have jokes explained to her. But she was also indifferent to most of the tricks of paradox, ambiguity, understatement and saying the opposite of what you mean, which pepper the talk of almost everyone else in this country."

Boris is the polar opposite. His mind is constantly darting around from register to register, in search of the joke or the device that explodes some strongly-held convention.

In this collection, you'll see how he constantly plays around with words for comic effect. That doesn't just mean looking for the most obscure or Wodehousian synonym. He also plays with the words themselves, as when he describes "The Tuscan palazzo of Count Girolamo Strozzi where Tony Blair forged one of New Labour's few hard-edged ideological positions: he was pro-sciutto and anti-pasto."

He played a similar trick in a speech praising the Education Secretary, noticing that his surname lent itself to verbal trickery: he *gove* us free schools, he *gove* us freedom from government control of schools.

The keen classicist Boris is also constantly shifting register between plain, simple Anglo-Saxon words and more complex, pompous Latinate ones.

He expanded on this art in 2007 at a Latin-themed charity evening at the rectory in East Sussex belonging to the former editor of the *Telegraph*, Charles Moore. I was speaking, too, at the event. Just like the more nervous quizmasters on *Have I Got News For You?*, I had spent several days rehearsing my speech – on 'The Joy of Latin'. Boris arrived late, in a cab that had come all the way from the Tory Conference in Blackpool he'd just addressed.

The audience were already in a state of presumption of hilarity, as Stephen Robinson called the Johnson effect. But they went into feverish levels of laughter when he actually started to talk, off the cuff, on the apparently dry topic of the use of Latinate words in English.

"The thing about Latinate words is they're evasive," said Boris, "There's a whole world of difference between 'You're sacked' and 'We want to restructure the whole operation in the M4 corridor'. Alan Clark used the device to brilliant effect in the Scott Inquiry. 'I was economical with the actualité' isn't just brilliant – it's also less self-condemnatory than 'I lied.'"

"You can see the effect at work in *Apocalypse Now* in the scene where they're discussing what to do with Colonel Kurtz, the Marlon Brando character."

Boris proceeded to recite the script from memory:

CIVILIAN: You'll go up the Nung River in a Navy PBR – appear at Nu Mung Ba as if by accident, re-establish your acquaintance with Colonel Kurtz, find out what's happened – and why. Then terminate his command.

WILLARD: Terminate?

CIVILIAN: Terminate with extreme prejudice.

"Now that last bit," continued Boris, "is a terrific bit of Latinate English. 'Terminate with extreme prejudice' is a much more elusive order than 'Kill him.'"

He also understands the comic power of shifting between the Latinate and Anglo-Saxon registers. Through his studies of what he calls the "crunchy" linguistics of Latin and Greek, Boris learnt to examine the building blocks of English up close.

As Evelyn Waugh said of his own classical education, he learnt "that words have basic inalienable meanings, departure from which is either conscious metaphor or inexcusable vulgarity." Boris knows exactly when to depart from those meanings to produce metaphor or vulgarity, and sometimes both at the same time.

When describing the location of his office in City Hall – "I'm on the, er, upper epidermis of the gonad. Somewhere near the seminal vesical,

I expect" – the joke depends on using the formal, scientific, Latinate terms for effect. We are more used to Anglo-Saxon terms being used for vulgarity and swear words – they become much funnier when formalised into technical, medical language.

Boris also often flicks between the two registers of high, classical art and low, juicy blockbuster for contrasted comic effect.

"He has an incredible memory," says his biographer, Andrew Gimson, "and he combines the low-brow with the high-brow – he loves extremely violent films."

His favourite film is the Ben Stiller vehicle, *Dodgeball*. When he says he identifies with the *Incredible Hulk* – "the madder Hulk gets, the stronger Hulk gets" – he knows whereof he speaks.

Depending on the occasion, he'll cherry-pick from his high- and low-brow memory banks. A few years ago, I remember coming across an extremely serious, erudite article by him on Horace in the *Spectator* – no jokes, no *Incredible Hulk* references. What was going on?

It was only when I got to the end that I saw the article had been taken from a speech he'd given to Oxford classics dons. Again, he was calibrating – up against the top brains, he jettisoned the trashy references. The cleverer Hulk's audience, the cleverer Hulk gets.

Even when he's apparently dropping down an intellectual notch or two, the brainpower is still churning away below the surface. Charles Moore noticed the intellect being smuggled in like this, in a 2002 *Telegraph* article by Boris. In it, the then Henley MP recalled being pelted with a bread roll by a Labour councillor at the Mayor of Henley's annual dinner.

Boris opened the article by describing the arc of the bread roll as it sailed over the banqueting tables of Henley Town Hall. Leaving the roll frozen in mid-air, he turned to the serious meat of his column – some obscure aspect of Tory policy. And then, as the article came to an end, he returned to the flight of the "mini French baguette".

Boris later admitted to Charles Moore that he was consciously using an ancient rhetorical device, much favoured by the Roman orator and politician, Cicero. The trick is called digressio, where you turn to a secondary, diverting story, while leaving your exciting original story hanging in mid-air – literally, in this case. In order to learn what happened to the bread roll, we read on in suspense, our appetite whetted, waiting for the mini-baguette to hit the blond fright wig – as indeed it did.

I have in fact been operating my own form of digressio in this introduction. I began by saying that my chat with Boris at his sister's launch party partly unpacks his character. Only now have I got round to the unpacking.

"Boris," I said that evening, "I've got to write an introduction to your collected wit and wisdom. I was just wondering whether you ever use any classical devices in your speeches or your articles."

"Oh yes, I most certainly do," he said, slipping on his ultra-serious skin, "There's one particular Roman oratorical trick I use the whole time. Couldn't survive without it."

"Oh really. What is it?"

"It's absolutely crucial – it's called imbecilio."

There, in a nutshell, is Johnsonian wit: the overstated plea to seriousness, with the rug pulled out from under it by over-advertised stupidity. Those Wodehousian one-liners – or one-off words, like imbecilio – are also much harder to create than you might think. As Evelyn Waugh said of Wodehouse, "One has to admire a man as a Master who can produce on average three uniquely brilliant and entirely original similes to every page."

Boris may not manage three per page; but there's usually at least one per article.

I wish Sebastian Faulks the best of luck in his Wodehouse sequel, *Jeeves and the Wedding Bells*, to be published this November. But I fear he won't be as good as Boris at Wodehousian simile, let alone as good as the Master.

And yet Boris pumps out the one-liners with apparent ease. In his Tory Conference speech in 2012, they came thick and fast: "the Ho Chi Minh trail into Hackney", the "giant hormonal valve" that opened up our souls during the Olympics to a wave of happiness, and the "charismatic megafauna in the Serengeti", as he referred to London's new double-deckers.

If you try to pick apart the building blocks of Boris's style – as I have unavoidably done while editing this book – you do see a certain amount of classical inspiration. It's most apparent in his extremely easy-going, colloquial style. He can only produce that breeziness by knowing the English language inside out.

That facility is largely to do with having studied classics. I would say that, as a fellow classicist, wouldn't I? But I noticed the same pattern when I was in charge of work-experience schoolchildren and graduates on the *Telegraph* Comment desk a few years ago. Most of them – whether they were educated privately or not – had pretty ropey grammar, and would invariably make at least one mistake in a paragraph. The classicists never did – once you've learnt the genitive case, you never get the grocer's apostrophe wrong again.

Boris lays a few classical idioms on top of that pleasing, flowing style, particularly anacoluthon – the sudden change of syntax in a sentence. He has even created his own form of anacoluthon

– faux-ignorant anacoluthon you might call it; suddenly breaking up his sentences to attack his own thought process: "As I was saying – what was I saying? – can someone tell me what I was saying?"

That said, it would be wrong to think of Johnsonian prose as just a cut-and-paste job of classical rhetoric.

As Andrew Gimson told me, "He'll know the classical names of oratorical devices but he hasn't got the aridity to be an academic classicist. He learnt everything he knows by the age of 11 or 12, from Clive Williams, his prep-school master. After that, his teachers just couldn't get him to work. The story goes that, at Oxford, he went and cried alone in a cinema when he failed to get a First. But the truth of it is that he didn't do nearly enough work. Even an hour a week would have been enough, but he didn't do even that."

Anyone who's taught Boris has been dazzled by his wit and memory, but disappointed by his capacity for long, concentrated periods of work. I once asked one of his old Oxford classics tutors about Boris's chances of making it to Downing Street.

"Capax imperii nisi imperasset..." said the old tutor, quoting the Roman historian Tacitus on the Emperor Galba: "He was up to the job of emperor as long as he never became emperor."

I'm not sure he's right – the qualities needed to get a First at Oxford, or send your copy in on time to the Deputy Comment Editor of the *Daily Telegraph*, are not the same required to get through the door of Number 10.

The people who swot for a First or get their article in by four o'clock don't have the touch of wildness, of comic anarchy, that makes an article or speech that much funnier – nor do they develop such a popular appeal as a result.

That appeal – and his comic gifts – were never better illustrated than at the 2012 Tory conference. He was greeted like a blond Messiah at Birmingham New Street Station by an impromptu mob of activists, crying, "Bo-ris! Bo-ris!"

No other politician gets that sort of unrehearsed reception – outside the conference hall, at least. And it's not just Conservative activists who feel that way. A friend of mine, watching the Olympics opening ceremony in an earthy pub in Leith, Edinburgh's port, was astounded to hear dyed-in-the-wool Scots Nationalist former dockers singing the same song: "Bo-ris! Bo-ris!"

The next day, in the conference hall, he crammed his speech with Borisisms. In praising Toby Young's new free school in west London – where all the pupils learn Latin – Boris dropped in an apparent aside about David Cameron not knowing the English for Magna Carta; he had been quizzed about it on the David Letterman show in New York.

Boris followed up with an improvised, "I know you knew it anyway", directed at the Prime Minister, who was sitting in the audience. A classic bit of Boris: a jokey criticism, disguised in a compliment, and still leaving behind the imprint of that underlying criticism.

Much of the speech was improvised. Frankie Howerd may have scripted his every titter-ye-not and ooh-missus, but Boris's asides jump out of the ether as he talks – which is handy, given he's not one for in-depth preparation. As Stuart Reid says, you can see the comic light flick on in his eyes; and he then makes a split-second decision whether to deploy the – possibly too risqué – gag that has instantly formed in his mind.

Politicians' jokes are usually telegraphed from a long distance – you sense them coming a mile off; you feel the hours of rehearsal with the crack team of policy wonk humourists in the previous months.

When Boris's one-liners come off the cuff, they are that much funnier for it.

Not that all his wit and wisdom are impromptu. Like all comedians, he relies on a shifting mass of familiar one-liners that he can slot in to fill gaps and answer awkward questions. On being asked whether he is planning to become Prime Minister, he has, on several occasions, said he is more likely to be reincarnated as an olive. One of his favourite words is dolichocephalic – meaning "long-headed"; his hero, Pericles, had an acute case of dolichocephalia.

Not everyone falls for this combination of rhetorical skills. One senior journalist has called him "a demagogue and rabble-rouser" for the way he manipulates a crowd. He's got a point. Look at Boris when he's waving his arms in the air to fire up an audience, and he is almost literally rousing the rabble. But, at the same time, the other Boris is toiling away – the stand-up comedian, hamming up the rabble-rouser role. And so he's saved from any accusation of egomania and narcissism by the self-mockery.

Egomaniacs and narcissists also tend to be over-protective of their reputation to an obsessive degree. Not Boris – he's too self-confident, and busy, to spend much time managing his PR. He showed a characteristic generosity of spirit, both in letting this book go ahead, and in having no desire to interfere with it, let alone bowdlerise it.

I'm extremely grateful to Robin Baird-Smith of Bloomsbury, for commissioning me to edit the book, with a similar generosity of spirit, and finances. Charles FitzRoy was very generous, too, in coming up with the idea and then letting me do it.

William Vignoles did an enormous amount of impressive work in tracking down Borisisms, from childhood to adulthood, from the *Wall Street Journal* to aperçus on the canvassing trail in deepest Oxfordshire. Many thanks to Kim Storry at Fakenham Prepress, and to Joel Simons and all at Bloomsbury.

Many thanks to the editors of the *Daily Telegraph* and the *Spectator*, and HarperCollins, for permission to quote from their publications.

Stuart Reid, Daniel Hannan, Christopher Howse, Jonathan Ford, James Fletcher, Rachel Johnson, Andrew Hobson, my parents and Andrew Gimson were extremely generous with their time, and their anecdotes. It is one of the easy joys of writing about Boris Johnson that, when you mention his name to anyone who's met him, the stories come out fully-formed, coherent and funny.

Harry Mount
Kentish Town, London NW5
April 2013

1

THE CHILD IS FATHER OF THE MAN – EARLY LIFE, ETON, OXFORD AND THE BULLINGDON

"Boo to grown ups!"

Boris's earliest surviving article, written on a wall in the Johnson family farm at Nethercote, Somerset, c.1969.

"As the oldest, I've always known that my position was basically unchallengeable. It is the fixed point about which my cosmos is organised.

1

I smile indulgently on everybody else's attempt to compete with me. Bring it on, I say."

Boris asserts his dominance to his sister, Julia.

"Me and my brothers and sisters are like the honey you used to get – produce of more than one country."

To Michael Cockerell, BBC, March 25, 2013.

"An actress could be a euphemism, we may be about to turn up a prostitute here. Not that I mind. I want you to know they can get up to anything, my ancestors, they have carte blanche to commit whatever acts of fornication they want as far as I'm concerned, but I want to know."

On revelations in the BBC's *Who Do You Think You Are* [2008] that he is descended from the illegitimate child of the actress Friederike Margrethe Porth (1776–1860).

"My life was one of blameless, panda-like passivity until my sister arrived 18 months later."

To Michael Cockerell, BBC, March 25, 2013.

"I tell you this. The Civilised World can ignore, must ignore entirely, these idiots who tell us that, by their very existence, the public schools demolish all hopes most cherished for the Comprehensive System. Clearly, this is twaddle, utter bunkum, balderdash, tommyrot, piffle and fiddlesticks of the most insidious kind. So strain every nerve, parents of Britain, to send your son to this educational establishment (forget the socialist gibberish about the destruction of the state system). Exercise your freedom of choice because, in this way, you will imbue your son with the most important thing, a sense of his own importance."

In defence of public schools, *The Eton Chronicle*,
December 12, 1980.

"I was a colossal swot of course, and I urge anyone listening to this programme to be a colossal swot. It's the only way forward."

On his success at Eton and Oxford.

"I do remember Dave. Someone said to me once, 'That's Cameron mi' and there was this tiny chap, I dimly remember."

On David Cameron at Eton, to Michael Cockerell, BBC, March 25, 2013.

"I'm terribly, terribly sorry. I've been so busy I just didn't have time to put in the mistakes."

On being accused by his Balliol tutor of lifting a Greek translation from a text book, c.1985.

"The terrible art of the candidate is to coddle the self-deception of the stooge."

How to attract support while campaigning for the presidency of the Oxford Union, *The Oxford Myth* [ed. Rachel Johnson, 1988].

"Like all harrowing and shattering defeats, it was very good for me."

On losing the election to become the Oxford Union President. He won the following year.

"A truly shameful vignette of almost super-human undergraduate arrogance, toffishness and twittishness. But at the time you felt it was wonderful to be going round, swanking it up. Or was it? Actually I remember the dinners being incredibly drunken. The abiding memory is of deep, deep self-loathing."

On the Bullingdon, to Michael Cockerell, BBC, March 25, 2013.

"Buller, Buller, Buller."

Boris's traditional greeting on meeting a fellow member of
the Bullingdon.

"Some time in my late teens I found myself in a
student house when someone put on *Start Me Up*
by the Rolling Stones. I am fully aware of what
sophisticated people are supposed to think about
those first three siren-jangling chords. But the
noise that came out of the battered old tape deck
seemed to vibrate in my rib cage. Something in
my endochrine system gave a squirt and pow, I
could feel myself being transformed from this shy,
spotty swotty nerd who had spent the past hour
trying to maintain a conversation with the poor
woman who was sitting next to me...

It was pure Jekyll and Hyde. It was Clark Kent
in the phone kiosk. I won't say that I leapt to my
feet and beat my chest and took the girl by the
hand. But I can't rule it out, because frankly I
can't remember the details, except that it involved
us all dancing on some chests of drawers and
smashing some chairs.

It was Keith I practically aimed to emulate
at the age of about 16 when I bought a pair of
tight purple cords (a sheen of sweat appears on
my brow as I write these words) and tried with

fat and fumbling fingers to plink out Satisfaction on a borrowed guitar; and my abysmal failure to become a rock star only deepened my hero worship."

On Keith Richards, Johnson's *Life of London* [2011].

"What a sharp-elbowed, thrusting and basically repellent lot we were. We were always bragging or shafting each other, and in a way we still are, with our pompous memoirs and calculated indiscretions."

On his Oxford contemporaries, *Spectator*, October 25, 2006.

"My original ambition was to become a billionaire proprietor of a multiple retail empire and the Jimmy Goldsmith of my generation. Something went wrong."

Boris's contribution to Dominic Sheldermine's *My Original Ambition* [2004].

"World king."

> Boris's ambition, according to his sister, Rachel.

"To achieve more notches on my phallocratic phallus."

> On his ambition, Eton leavers' book, 1982.

IN THE WORDS OF OTHERS

"Alexander Boris weighed 9 pounds 1 ounce at birth and is a remarkably lusty child."

> Stanley Johnson reports the birth of his son to Boris Litwin, a friend and benefactor who Boris is named after.

"Wilfully scruffy."

> William Mostyn-Owen, father of Boris's first wife,
> Allegra, on his future son-in-law.

"No Prussian militarist with a bankrupt estate in

the barren depths of Brandenburg could be more single-minded than Boris in pursuit of knock-out victory."

Andrew Gimson, his biographer.

"If anyone is coming top in the Johnson league table, it would be the one my father refers to as: 'Boris, that great prodigious tree in the rainforest, in the shade of which the smaller trees must either perish or struggle to find their own place in the sun.'"

His sister, Julia Johnson.

"There was always tremendous competition to climb trees higher, or learn to read first. I think the last time I beat Boris at anything was when I won the Scottish dancing prize at the age of twelve. It's been a rapid ascent for him ever since. He planted his flag first on the summit of so many Mount Olympuses that we younger siblings have to content ourselves in tooling quietly around the foothill of our own careers."

Rachel Johnson.

"Boris really has adopted a disgracefully cavalier attitude to his classical studies ... Boris sometimes seems affronted when criticised for what amounts to a gross failure of responsibility (and surprised at the same time that he was not appointed Captain of the School for next half): I think he honestly believes that it is churlish of us not to regard him as an exception, one who should be free of the network of obligation which binds everyone else."

April 1982 school report by Martin Hammond, Eton housemaster and classics master.

"Hey, hey, ABJ! How many Oppidans did you kill today? Watch the Blond Behemoth crud relentlessly through the steaming pile of purple-and-orange heavyweights, until he is knocking on the Lower-Master's door."

Wall Game report, *The Eton Chronicle*, 1983.

"He had a great rivalry with Kabir Nath. There were two genius musicians in my year. Paul

Richardson won the piano competition every year, except one year when Kabir Nath got it. Boris found this insufferable. He took up the piano, thinking he'd win it next year. He had no idea how difficult the piano was. He had such confidence in his own ability he just thought he'd come sailing in."

School friend, Andrew Gilmour.

"There was a dividing line between tutors who liked Boris the Great and those who disliked him. His disarming frankness was his ultimate weapon."

Jasper Griffin, professor of Classical Literature at Balliol.

"If I added up the IQ of my father and my mother, don't you think they'd be more than the IQ of your father and mother."

To his first wife, Allegra Mostyn-Owen.

2

BORIS'S NINE LIVES: GAFFES, DENIALS AND RESURRECTIONS

"I will greatly miss Alan Johnson, not just because he is a nice guy but also for the satisfaction I used to get when I saw a headline saying, 'Johnson in new gaffe' and realised it wasn't me.'"

On Alan Johnson standing down as Shadow Chancellor of the Exchequer, January 20, 2011.

"As a general tactic in life, it is often useful to give the slight impression that you are deliberately pretending not to know what is going on – because the reality may be that you don't know what's going on, but people won't be able to tell the difference."

To Michael Cockerell, BBC, March 25, 2013.

Boris's gaffe-prone reputation began early – he was fired from the *Times* graduate training scheme for making up a quotation. He made the error in a report, on May 24, 1988, about the possible discovery of Edward II's Rosary Palace, falsely attributing it to his godfather, Dr Colin Lucas, of Balliol College, Oxford:

"Archaeologists working on an urban development site on the South Bank of the Thames have discovered the long-lost palace of King Edward II. They have also found the remains of the large house of Sir John Fastog, thought to be the model for the Shakespearean character of Sir John Falstaff.

A large stone corner of the royal palace, built in about 1325, first came to light at the Hay's Wharf site last week, but excavators have tried to keep the discovery quiet because of the danger of attracting treasure hunters... The palace was a large moated building, about 80 yards square. Known to historians as the 'Rosary', it was a retreat on the far side of the river where the king could escape the cares of office.

According to Dr Colin Lucas, of Balliol College, Oxford, this is where the king enjoyed a reign of dissolution with his catamite, Piers Gaveston, before he was gruesomely murdered at Berkeley Castle by barons who felt he was too prone to foreign influence."

He also included some rather spurious speculation about Sir John Fastog:

"The discovery near the house of riverfront installations suggests that Sir John was quite unlike the rumbustious devil-may-care Shakespearean character."

It turned out that Boris had rung up Lucas and asked him about Edward II. Lucas answered with a few general observations about Edward II's reign and the relationship with Piers Gaveston. Boris had then fabricated a terrible howler and attributed it to Lucas – Gaveston was executed in 1312, 13 years before the palace was supposedly built. Boris was forced to rewrite the story four days later.

In an interview with the *Independent* in 2002, he said of the episode: "It was a complete nightmare of a disaster, and to make it even worse, that very week, Colin was trying to become Master of Balliol College. He later succeeded – but not that time. Of all the mistakes I've made, I think that takes the biscuit."

"I mildly sandpapered something somebody said."

On making up the Edward II quote. To Eddie Mair, BBC, March 24, 2013.

"It's great to be here, folks. It's absolutely wonderful to be here in Manchester, one of the few great British cities I have yet to insult."

Boris takes the stage at the Conservative Party Conference, October 5, 2009.

"This programme was such a bad idea."

To Michael Cockerell, BBC, March 25, 2013.

Accusation of racism:

"It is said that the Queen has come to love the Commonwealth, partly because it supplies her with regular cheering crowds of flag-waving picaninnies; and one can imagine that Blair, twice victor abroad but enmired at home, is similarly seduced by foreign politeness. They say he is shortly off to the Congo. No doubt the AK47s will fall silent, and the pangas will stop their hacking of human flesh, and the tribal warriors will all break out in watermelon smiles to see the big white chief touch down in his big white British taxpayer-funded bird."

Daily Telegraph, January 10, 2002. Boris apologised for the article six years later when standing for Mayor of London.

Operation Scouse Grovel:

In October 2004, Michael Howard ordered Boris to make a penitential visit to Liverpool after an unsigned editorial, written by Simon Heffer, was published in the *Spectator* about the murder of the engineer Ken Bigley in Iraq:

"The extreme reaction to Mr Bigley's murder is fed by the fact that he was a Liverpudlian. Liverpool is a handsome city with a tribal sense of community. A combination of economic misfortune – its docks were, fundamentally, on the wrong side of England when Britain entered what is now the European Union – and an excessive predilection for welfarism have created a peculiar, and deeply unattractive, psyche among Liverpudlians. They see themselves whenever possible as victims, and resent their victim status; yet at the same time they wallow in it.

Part of this flawed psychological state is that they cannot accept that they might have made any contribution to their misfortunes, but seek rather to blame someone else for it, thereby deepening their sense of shared tribal grievance against the rest of society.

The deaths of more than 50 Liverpool supporters at Hillsborough in 1989 was undoubtedly a greater tragedy than the single death, however horrible, of Mr Bigley; but that is no excuse Liverpool's failure to acknowledge, even to this day, the part played in the disaster by drunken fans at the back of the crowd who mindlessly tried to fight their way into the ground that Saturday afternoon.

The police became a convenient scapegoat, and the *Sun* newspaper a whipping-boy for daring, albeit in a tasteless fashion, to hint at the wider causes of the incident."

Boris attempted to clear things up in his *Telegraph* column, agreeing that elements the leader were tasteless and ill-judged, while adding that he stood by some of the points made:

"I can't remember what words Paul Bigley [the victim's brother] used to describe me yesterday afternoon, on the line to a BBC studio, but I think he said I was 'a self-centred, pompous twit'. He wanted to say how much he disliked my appearance, my voice, my mannerisms, and how much he wished I would just disappear.

No matter how big your ego, there is something crushing in being so addressed, not just because I have never met Paul Bigley, but also because he has just suffered an appalling bereavement, and is the object of national sympathy.

'How do you feel?' they all asked, when I left the studio. 'Do you feel bad?' asked the girls and lads with the cameras and the notebooks.

The answer was that I felt winded, drained by a sudden proximity to personal suffering and grief. I felt like Police Chief Brodie in Jaws, slapped round the face by the mother of the little kid killed by the shark.

There was nothing I could really say, except to repeat what we said in last week's leader in the *Spectator*: that we had extended our maximum sympathy to him and his family.

Just as I was recovering from this encounter, I found myself sitting next to a survivor of the Hillsborough tragedy, and it may not surprise you to know that he took much the same view of me as Paul Bigley had, and that this was also pretty shattering.

You have good days, and less good days, and yesterday was one of the less good days. There are those who say that I should not have gone, and that it was unnecessary for the *Spectator* to apologise for the tiniest fraction of its leading article. We should have stuck to our guns, people tell me, and to hell with Liverpool and to hell with the Tory leadership.

Well, I am not so sure. It is true that there were plenty of people who were warm, and welcoming, and kind. There was the man in the park who was out for his morning run, wearing a tracksuit, who hailed me with the words: 'Oi Boris, never mind the bollocks, a lot of what you said was true.' There was the Scouser at the airport who said, as he frisked me, that he agreed with every word of it.

But, in between, there were dozens and dozens of people who showed every sign of genuine hurt and incomprehension. Why did we make these cruel generalisations about welfare-addicted Liverpudlians?

Why had we felt it necessary to drag in the Bigley family's tragedy? Above all, why had we got our facts wrong about Hillsborough?

Of course, if I were simply an editor, and not an MP as well, I would have brushed it all off with a few phrases, nicely done up in an all-purpose letter of semi-apology, and asked my secretary to pp the letters. I would have remained behind the wonderful garden wall of journalism, able to chuck my rocks with no thought for the tinkling of the greenhouse.

But having been to Liverpool, and having been eyeball to glistering eyeball with those who felt they deserved an apology, I am glad I went, and I think at least some of them are a bit glad that I went, too.

I was able to say sorry for causing offence, and sorry for any hurt done to the Bigley family, and sorry for having reopened old wounds over Hillsborough, and that, in so far as we inaccurately represented the characteristics of the Liverpudlians, by resorting to some tired old stereotypes, I was sorry for that, too.

There are some who say that it was outrageous that Johnson the editor should have been ordered to eat humble pie by Michael Howard. But they miss the point, that I was already consuming large quantities of humble pie before Michael made his suggestion, that any editor would have felt obliged to make some amends for that article – in view of the outrage that was provoked – and that, in any event, Johnson the politician apologises for and refuses to apologise for exactly the same things as Johnson the editor."

Daily Telegraph, October 21, 2004.

"The quality of Mersey is not strained."

His response when the people of Liverpool forgave him,
December 2, 2005.

"Mayoral culpa, mayoral maxima culpa."

On calling a St Patrick's Day gala dinner 2012
"Lefty crap".

Other places Boris has insulted:

"In the Tory Party we have become used to Papua New Guinea-style orgies of cannibalism and chief-killing, and so it is with a happy amazement that we watch as the madness engulfs the Labour party."

Boris on the Labour leadership chaos, *Daily Telegraph*, September 8, 2006.

"I mean no insult to the people of Papua New Guinea who I'm sure lead lives of blameless bourgeois domesticity in common with the rest of us. I'm happy to add Papua New Guinea to my global itinerary of apology."

"One of the most depressed towns in southern England, a place that is arguably too full of drugs, obesity, underachievement and Labour MPs."

On Portsmouth, GQ, 2007.

ON SEX

The exposure of Boris's affair with Petronella Wyatt sparked his dismissal from the Shadow

Cabinet after he categorically denied its existence in the *Mail on Sunday*, on November 7, 2004:

"I have not had an affair with Petronella. It is complete balderdash. It is an inverted pyramid of piffle. It is all completely untrue and ludicrous conjecture. I am amazed that people can write this drivel."

It turned out to be true, and Boris was dismissed for lying about the affair. He still tried to inject some levity into the situation:

"I did not mislead Michael Howard. I advise you all very strongly, go for a run, get some exercise, and have a beautiful day."

Boris to waiting journalists in the wake of his sacking. He later added Dr Pangloss's words from Candide, "All is for the best in the best of all possible worlds."

"I said, 'Sack me or sack me.'"

To Michael Howard on lying over the Petronella Wyatt affair, to Michael Cockerell, BBC, March 25, 2013.

"I am sorry this decision has been taken in response to stories about my private life. I am looking forward to helping promote a new Conservative policy on the arts, and I will continue to do my utmost to serve the people of Henley and south Oxfordshire. I am now going to have a stiff drink."

The note Boris distributed to friends in the wake of his dismissal.

"I'd recommend getting ignominiously sacked – and I want you to know that I insisted on my right to be sacked: 'Sack me,' I said, by way of an ultimatum because it is only by being sacked that you can truly engender sympathy. Nothing excites compassion, in friend and foe alike, as much as the sight of you ker-splonked on the Tarmac with your propeller buried six feet under... My friends, as I have discovered myself, there are no disasters, only opportunities. And, indeed, opportunities for fresh disasters."

On being sacked from the Tory front bench, *Daily Telegraph*, December 2, 2004.

"I told Boris I don't care what he does in his private life and he told me, 'Nor do I.'"

Then *Telegraph* editor Charles Moore in the wake of the Wyatt affair.

"He always looked like he'd just got out of bed and apparently he had."

Dan Colson, former chief executive of the Telegraph Group.

"Women cannot resist men who obviously like women."

"I haven't had to have a wank for 20 years."

Boris to a friend.

The antics of Boris and others at the "Sextator" – including Kimberly Fortier, the *Spectator* publisher who had an affair with then-Home Secretary David Blunkett – were turned into a play. *Who's the Daddy?* was written by the magazine's theatre critics, Toby Young and Lloyd Evans. Boris was the lead character, often clad in tiger-print boxers:

"Come on, Petsy, nothing like a good scrum after lunch!"

The Boris character, as he seduces Petronella in a broom cupboard.

"I don't know whether I'll have time to catch it before it closes."

The real Boris on whether he was planning to see the play.

"A place of monastic seclusion."

On the *Spectator*, at the *Spectator* Christmas lunch, December 16, 2004.

"No one who has done it can forget the semi-sexual sense of release when the electronic moaning and squeaking indicated that the article had arrived."

On sending articles down the telephone line, 1987.

"I imagine it is like being asked to make love to a woman who has just achieved bliss in the arms of Errol Flynn, or Robin Cook, or someone."

On following Ann Widdecombe as a speaker at a
Conservative event.

"Come on, man: stop being so indescribably wet. If she's so beautiful, standing there in your T-shirt and floppy fringe, and hush your hopeless falsetto crooning. Go out and get her, is my advice."

On the James Blunt song, "You're Beautiful".

3

FOURTH ESTATE
BORIS – TRIUMPH
IN BRUSSELS, THE
SPECTATOR YEARS

"There were two of us who were taken on as trainees in the late eighties, and it was him or me who was going to get the job at the end of the eight or nine months. It was mano a mano, and of course it was him who got it."

On his failure at *The Times*, Desert Island Discs,
October 30, 2005.

"I was sort of chucking these rocks over the garden wall and I listened to this amazing crash from the greenhouse next door over in England as everything I wrote from Brussels was having this amazing, explosive effect on the Tory Party. And it really gave me this, I suppose, rather weird sense of power."

On his time in Brussels for the *Daily Telegraph*, Desert Island Discs, October 2005.

"Homo Foederalis."

On Jacques Delors.

"[My position switched from] a position of moderate idealism to one of vinegarish scepticism."

On his changing views on Europe during his time in Brussels.

"I used to interview people. Terribly difficult. You have a wonderful time with this chap, or girl, end up with a dumper truck of gravel from which you pick shiny pebbles to make your mosaic. It's seduction and betrayal."

Radio Times, September 2004.

"How badly are you going to hurt this guy?... OK, Darry, I've said I'll do it, I'll do it."

To Darius Guppy who asked Boris for the contact details
of a reporter he wanted beaten up.

The *Spectator* years...

"I'm hard at it, transforming the *Spectator* into a McVitie biscuit. What I mean is an opening of solid meal, followed suddenly and dramatically by a chocolate taste explosion."

On his plans for the magazine to its then owner,
Conrad Black.

"The blessed sponge of amnesia has wiped the chalkboard of history."

To the *New York Times*, when asked about his broken promise not to edit the *Spectator* and to run for Parliament, April 2002.

"The horses are starting to get further and further apart, and the straddling operation is becoming increasingly stressful on the crotch region."

On how he juggled the roles of being MP for Henley with the editorship of the *Spectator*, 2004.

"In spite of all our efforts to shake off readers, they continue to subscribe to us in ever greater numbers."

Christmas speech to the *Spectator* staff, December 16, 2004, Berry Bros & Rudd, St James's.

"For most of my time here, I have been propelled by your talents, as a fat German tourist may be transported by superior alpinists to the summit of Everest."

Farewell speech to *Spectator* staff, December 15, 2005, Franco's Restaurant, Jermyn Street.

Others on Boris at the *Times*, and in Brussels:

"We were chalk and cheese – he, breathlessly posh and educated in the classics, me a hardened hack who had left school at 16 to become a trainee reporter on my local paper in Romford – but I took to the guy. For anyone with a penchant for dishevelled English eccentrics, it was hard not to."

David Sapsted, later news editor of the *Telegraph*, took Boris under his wing when he arrived at the *Times* as a graduate trainee in 1989.

"Over the next few years, he developed the persona which has become famous today, a facade resembling that of Gussie Fink-Nottle, allied to wit, charm, brilliance and startling flashes of instability."

Max Hastings, the *Telegraph* editor who appointed Boris to Brussels.

"He was already part of the establishment, friends with Lord Spencer and so on and consequently he saw journalists as birds of carrion rather than fine upstanding, investigative types. He never did the investigative thing or proper news. And he was always alive to money – money was very important to him. He was mixing with bankers, who saw the world as a business opportunity. So it was clear that he was never going to be just a passive observer, which is what the rest of us are. I think there was always in his mind the idea of going and doing something, to try and be part of public life. He was therefore very careful not to upset important people."

Quentin Letts, editor of the *Telegraph's* Peterborough column during Boris's time in Brussels.

"We answer his attacks, but the problem is that our answers are not funny."

An EU official on Boris's reportage.

4

BORIS IN THE HOUSE – POLITICAL VIEWS

"I tend to remember things like whether they had dung on their foreheads, or whether they told me a recipe for making brandy by boiling up Weetabix and blackcurrants."

On whether he remembered constituents' names and faces, during his failed attempt to gain the Parliamentary seat for Clwyd South in 1997. As he put it, "I fought Clwyd South – and Clwyd South fought back."

"Look, I'm rather pro-European, actually. I certainly want a European community where one can go off and scoff croissants, drink delicious coffee, learn foreign languages and generally make love to foreign women."

Boris on the EU, during his failed first bid for parliament.

"The trouble with campaigning in the wilds of Oxfordshire is that you lose touch with the main battle. I feel lost in the jungle, way up the Nong River, 75 clicks beyond the Do Long bridge."

"Go back home and prepare for breakfast."

Victory speech, Henley 2001.

"Your car will go faster, your girlfriend will have a bigger bra size. It's an attested fact that, under Conservative governments, the quality of living of the British people has immeasurably improved, leading to better denticians, higher calcium consumption, leading inexorably to superior mammary development."

On voting Tory, GQ, May 2003.

"If Amsterdam or Leningrad vie for the title of Venice of the North, then Venice – what compliment is high enough? Venice, with all her civilisation and ancient beauty, Venice with her addiction to curious aquatic means of transport, yes, my friends, Venice is the Henley of the South."

On his constituency, *Daily Telegraph*, March 11, 2004.

"If you don't go out and mix it up a bit on the stuff that everybody watches, if you don't get involved in things that everybody thinks are amusing and if you're not prepared to get involved in vernacular, real TV and you just stick on Andrew Neil's late-night yawn-a-thon, then you're never going to get anywhere."

On his appearances on TV programmes such as *Have I Got News For You* and *Top Gear*, in *GQ*, May 2003.

"Hello, hello, hello, I said to myself as I spotted something on the floor, what have we here? I was standing on the palm-fringed banks of the Tigris, in what had once been a gorgeous, spanking villa.

You never saw such a mess. Naked wires sprouted from every wall where the light fittings had been ripped out. The very bidets had been smashed by the mob, in search of heaven knows what, and the safe lay blackened and gaping on its side, apparently having been opened by a bazooka.

Everything of value or interest had been looted, or almost everything; because here on the floor was something so trodden on and covered with dust that it had perhaps gone unrecognised.

It was a fine red leather cigar case, capable of holding three Winston Churchills. It was located in the front hall of the villa of Tariq Aziz, a known lover of cigars. And therefore, unless I missed my guess, it was the cigar case of Tariq Aziz.

Instinctively, I reached down to snatch it up. Some journalists had rootled around in Baghdad and found sensational documents, appearing to incriminate Western politicians. It fell to your columnist to find a vital relic of our times, the object that nestled in the Iraqi foreign minister's breast pocket, and which was in some sense even closer to his heart than Saddam Hussein himself.

This cigar case had silently attended the innermost meetings of the Ba'ath Revolutionary Council. If ever Saddam had given away the secret location of his weapons of mass destruction, the chances are that this cigar case was in the room. That is why I picked it up; and I was just about to trouser it when a still, small voice said, hang on. It was true that no one else had shown the slightest respect for the goods and chattels of Tariq Aziz. To take the cigar case of the deposed number two of a deposed tyrant was hardly the same as swiping a 2300 BC bronze statue of a squatting Akkadian king."

On Tariq Aziz's cigar case, *Daily Telegraph*, May 1, 2003. Five years later, Scotland Yard asked Boris to hand over the case.

"The real shocker is not that people are foolish enough to appear on TV, but that people are so idle as to watch it."

"The dreadful truth is that when people come to see their MP, they have run out of better ideas."

Daily Telegraph, September 18, 2003.

"The Lib Dems are not just empty. They are a void within a vacuum surrounded by a vast inanition."

Daily Telegraph, September 2003.

"I find I don't have much difficulty getting people to listen to me seriously when I want to. And I'm not going to produce a series of spine-crackingly tedious pamphlets for the sake of gravitas. I think it's important to remember that most people find politics unbelievably dull, so I don't see any particular vice in trying to sugar the pill with a few jokes."

On his political approach, *Independent*, 2004.

"It is a sign of the decline of any great civilisation that its people begin to worship strange gods: one thinks of the late Roman interest in Egyptian man-jackals. Now we have a new divinity that commands the adoration of the governing classes, as nannying and multiple-bosomed as Diana of Ephesus. Her name is Phobia, and sacrifices are being made at her altar."

On the growth of health and safety, *Daily Telegraph*, October 7, 2004.

"Look, the point is... er, what is the point? It's a tough job but somebody's got to do it."

Boris on his elevation to shadow arts minister in 2004.

"Voting Tory will cause your wife to have bigger breasts and increase your chance of owning a BMW M3."

General election campaign, 2005.

"Hello, I'm your MP. Actually I'm not. I'm your candidate. Gosh."

Campaigning in Henley, 2005.

"I'm very attracted to it. I may be diverting from Tory party policy here, but I don't care."

On proposed 24-hour licensing laws, interview in
The Times, 2005.

"I'm having Sunday lunch with my family. I'm vigorously campaigning, inculcating my children in the benefits of a Tory government."

Reply to being asked whether he was canvassing for the 2005 general election, the *Guardian*, April 11, 2005.

"Life isn't like coursework, baby. It's one damn essay crisis after another."

Daily Telegraph, May 12, 2005.

"My instincts are not to go around, trying to exterminate Mickey Mouse courses. One man's Mickey Mouse course is another man's literae humaniores."

In his first interview as Tory higher education spokesman, 2006.

"Ich bin ein Frankfurter."

Said in homage to the views on education held by Justice Felix Frankfurter, January 24, 2006.

"We are still the second most important country on Earth. The trick of maintaining such influence, of course, is to go around pretending to be very bumbling and hopeless and self-deprecating, a skill at which we excel."

"There's been something bizarre about the lip-smacking savagery of the new Liberal Democrats, with Vince Cable morphing into a mad axeman, a transformation as incongruous as the killer rabbit in Monty Python."

Conservative Party Conference, Manchester, 2009.

"There is a risk of us all starting to sound like a suicide cult."

On the dangers of the Conservatives' negative rhetoric on the economy, *The Andrew Marr Show*, 2009.

"I think that whatever type of Walls sausage that is contrived by this great experiment, the dominant ingredient has got to be Conservatism. The meat in the sausage has got to be Conservative."

On coalition negotiations, to Jeremy Paxman after the 2010 General Election.

"I was at the same school as the party leader. There we were at the same antiquated red brick establishment, with the famous old national waterway flowing nearby, and green playing fields of exceptional lushness just over the road, absolutely terrific. I was at the same North London primary school as Ed Miliband! I look at Ed and I think, 'where did it all go wrong?' His key selling point for the people of this country as a leader, is that he isn't Tony Blair. I looked at him and after a while I began to wish that he was."

On Ed Miliband, Tory Party Conference, September 2010.

"Shall I tell you the best thing about Jodhpur? It's not the old walled city and its picturesque markets and blissfully defecating cows. It's not even the fort of the Maharajahs, with its huge

46

pink barrels of stone soaring above the acropolis. It's the zipwire. Some British entrepreneurs have set up a series of zipwires that send you like Batman around the moats and the crenellations. It's stunning, and they are preparing to expand to other Indian cities. Just think: 99 per cent of Indians have never been on a plane — and the potential zipwire market is even bigger."

On his New Year's Eve, 2010, in Rajasthan, the *Spectator*, January 15, 2011.

"We cannot know what is going through the mind of crazed ex-despot Muammar Gaddafi as he continues to flee Nato bombs and rebel snipers – but we can have a good guess. He may be holed up gibbering in a basement in Sirte. He may be in Venezuela or working as a suspiciously taciturn short-order chef in a falafel bar in Tripoli.

Wherever he is I wager there is one thing that causes the old dyed ringlets to shake with rage, one thought that brings the foam to the corner of his champing jaws – and that is the treachery of all those he thought of as friends. And of those who have ratted on him in the last six months, there is one particular group of traitors that he would like to cast – I bet – to the nethermost fire-bubbling pit of hell. Never mind the rebels, and all those snaky ex-ministers who chose to defect as soon as the going got tough. Forget the buxom female 'bodyguards' who took the first plane back to Ukraine. For sheer duplicity there is no one to beat – the British! May the fleas of a thousand camels infest their armpits!

Gaddafi groans behind his dark glasses, pouring some hot sauce on the falafel. No wonder they talk about perfidious Albion, he mutters, and you can see why. It was only a few years ago that Tony Blair himself came out to his tent, almost snogged the Mad Dog, and proclaimed a new era of cooperation between Britain and Libya. The shooting of Yvonne Fletcher, the murder of hundreds of innocent people at Lockerbie — all appeared forgotten as ever grander emanations of the British state were despatched by London to slobber over the colonel's jackboots, and to help win oil contracts for British companies."

On Colonel Gaddafi, *Daily Telegraph*, September 5, 2011.

"It was only a few years ago that government ministers, and indeed politicians of all parties, were engaged in a protracted cringe before the wealth-generating power of the Masters of the Universe. And the bankers, in turn, became quite used to the flattery. They were put on important task forces to improve the governance of the country. They were given knighthoods for services to banking. They would sit at posh dinners with politicians beside them behaving in the manner, let us be frank, of some seductive courtesan. 'You so rich! Your hedge fund so massive! Me love you long time!'"

On the bankers, *Daily Telegraph*, September 5, 2011.

"Spending an hour with the FT is like being trapped in a room with assorted members of a millennialist suicide cult. If their pundits are to be believed, the skies of the City will shortly be dark with falling bankers, and then for the rest of us it's back to the 1930s, with barrels for trousers, soup kitchens and buddy can you spare a dime."

Daily Telegraph, October 14, 2011

"Happy birthday, by the way. I was pleased to see the other day that you have called me a blond-haired mop. A mop. Well, if I am a mop then you are a broom. A broom that is clearing up the mess left by the Labour government, and what a fantastic job you are doing. I thank you and congratulate you and your colleagues – George Osborne the dustpan, Michael Gove the J cloth, William Hague the sponge."

Boris addresses David Cameron, Conservative Party Conference, October 2012.

"We need to abandon the rhetoric of austerity, because if you endlessly tell businesses to tighten their belts and eat nut cutlets and drink their own urine, then you will be putting a big downer on growth and enterprise."

Speech to the CBI, November 2012.

"Chris Patten should make a penitential pilgrimage to McAlpine's Italian B&B, on his knees and scourging himself with a copy of the BBC charter."

On the *Newsnight* and Jimmy Savile scandals at the BBC.

"The hair-shirt, Stafford Cripps agenda is not the way to get Britain moving again."

Speech to the Davos Economic Forum, January 25, 2013.

"The Lib Dems are wobbling jellies of indecision and vacillation, particularly Clegg... His single contribution to politics has been to do a U-turn on tuition fees and make a song about it. That's all he's done... It is our constitutional duty to kick the Lib Dems in the – well, do they have any?"

On the Liberal Democrats, as he campaigned in the Eastleigh by-election, February 20, 2013.

"You just have to chuck a snowball into a cocktail party at Davos and you'd hit someone with a sovereign wealth fund who would fund a piece of infrastructure like that."

On how to fund enterprise projects such as a second Crossrail, longer tube lines, more river crossings and a new hub airport, Davos 2013.

"The hills and dales of Britain are being forested with white satanic mills, and yet the total contribution of wind power is still only about 0.4 per cent of Britain's needs. Wave power, solar power, biomass – their collective oomph wouldn't pull the skin off a rice pudding."

On green power, *Daily Telegraph*, December 14, 2009.

"There is something about human beings that means we are hard-wired to ignore intimations of mortality. Do you remember poor Ricky Ray Rector, the half-wit murderer who was executed in Arkansas in 1992? As is customary on Death Row, Ricky Ray was given a splendid last meal topped off with pecan pie. As he rose to take his farewell from the world, he told his guards that he hadn't finished the pecan pie but would 'save it for later'. That, I am afraid, is us.

With part of our minds, we may accept that we are in mortal danger. But we find it very hard to make the full imaginative leap. We may be told by thousands of scientists and environmentalists that we are about to fry – and we may be able to understand the case they make – but some deep instinct none the less urges us to believe, inductively, that things will go on more or less as they are. That is why the polls show such an amazingly obstinate public refusal to accept the reality of global warming."

On the Copenhagen climate change summit, *Daily Telegraph*, December 14, 2009.

"It was about 6am and a beautiful dawn was breaking as the captain drew our attention to an incredible sight on the starboard side. 'We're flying over Mount Kilimanjaro,' he said. I craned my neck and then gasped with horror. The last time I had seen the great mountain was 34 years ago. Today, the difference was obvious.

It was like seeing a beautiful film star without her wig on or stumbling on some famed international statesman in the nude. 'The snows are melting,' sighed a Tanzanian priest who happened to be standing next to me. 'They will never return.'"

On global warming, *Daily Telegraph*, August 30, 2010.

"It is not just that you can go there and see a carnival of animals and birds like nothing on earth – as though you were walking among the living relics of the Pleistocene. You also understand that there are still some places on the planet where you are not the top of the food chain. We were lucky to have our trip organised by a family called Fox, whose senior representative had been sent out in the 1950s to grow tea for Brooke Bond. On some nights, he would tell us stories of encounters with animals ('Fantastic, Mr Fox!' we would breathe). There was the hippo whose ivory sabres almost chopped one of his workers in half, spilling his guts.

There was the croc who pulled all the meat off the arm of another, like a chicken leg. 'We packed them both off to hospital patched them both up – and you know what, they didn't complain once. They were just happy to be alive.' He described a wonderful prelapsarian world in which he and his children would camp under the stars, with nothing but mosquito nets, or dive to retrieve fishing lures from croc-infested pools.

It was a Wilbur Smith Africa, innocent of elf and safety or ambulance-chasing lawyers. To a marvellous degree, in these safari camps, it still is.

There is the head waiter whose temples are scarred with the bite of a lion, and who still does his job perfectly in spite of losing two teaspoonfuls of brain."

On African health and safety, *Daily Telegraph*,
August 30, 2010.

"The gist of my plan (or so they seemed to think) was to commandeer super-ferries laden with unemployed Venusian layabouts, draw them up off the beaches at Ramsgate and Deal, and then open the bow doors and order the hordes to swarm ashore – scrounging benefits from under the noses of the indigenous people.

And then, they seemed to imagine, I was going to charter fleets of C-130s and parachute legions of destitute Martian bludgers over the Home Counties, on a mission to bivouac in the front rooms of Middle England, cooking goat curry on campfires made of broken-up domestic furniture and ruthlessly winning the affections of the daughters of the house."

On his plan to relax immigration, *Daily Telegraph*,
September 13, 2010.

"This is the column that leaps to the defence of the unfashionable cause. I once said the Serbs were not all bad. I have made a faint sheeplike defence of George W. Bush. I have stuck up for foxhunting and bankers and entered a general plea on behalf of all fat, white, male, hetero-sexual Tories who see nothing much wrong with drinking a bottle of wine at lunch and then having a quiet cigar.

In almost every case you would agree that there are at least some positive things that can be said for these characters — arguments that are at risk of being lost in the right-on hysteria. It is in that spirit that today I unsheath my columnar Excalibur and come to the aid of a great British company. It is time to speak up not just for the management and workforce of BP, but for everyone whose pension depends on BP shares — and that is a lot of people."

In the wake of the Deepwater Horizon disaster in the Gulf of Mexico, *Daily Telegraph*, September 17, 2012.

"The last time I looked, there were about seven billion people on this planet. There are all sorts of candidates for the Nobel Peace Prize. Across the developing world, you will find gaunt and patient aid workers who have consecrated their lives to ending tribal conflicts. There are bone-nosed eco-warriors who are fighting to save the peoples of the rainforest from destruction. There are women who are struggling for female emancipation in Saudi Arabia. In tyrannies from Uzbekistan to North Korea, there are journalists risking life so the truth can be heard. There are good people battling every scourge, from famine to gun running to human trafficking. So we can only wonder what madness took hold at the judging lunch the other day, when that committee of Norwegian worthies was asked to appoint this year's winner of the prize. Perhaps they were drunk; perhaps it was one of those morose Scandinavian afternoons when the sun has sunk and there is no alternative but to hit the aquavit. Whatever it was, they must have been out of their minds to ignore all human candidates and award the prize to the European Union."

On the EU winning the Nobel Peace Prize, *Daily Telegraph*, October 15, 2012.

"We have just seen cuts to school sports programmes – which you might have thought were an essential element of a sporting legacy from the 2012 Olympics – and this is the moment that the Commission seriously thinks it can come to the British taxpayer and ask for billions more in subsidy. My message to M van Rompuy is donnez-moi un break, mate. The people in Brussels must have been out of their tiny minds. It is like giving heroin to an addict. It is like handing an ice cream to the fattest boy in the class, while the rest of the kids are on starvation diets – and then asking him to pay for his treat."

On proposed increases to the EU's budget, *Daily Telegraph*, November 19, 2012.

"He [Lord Justice Leveson] seems to want to make the British press as earnest as the *Neue Zürcher Zeitung*, whose front-page splash was once about '100 years of Electric Light in Switzerland'."

On the Leveson report, 2012.

"This year, yet again, Andy Murray reached the last 16 at Wimbledon, along with players from Germany, France, America, Russia, Spain, Argentina, Croatia, Switzerland, Uzbekistan and Serbia. And once again it was Murray who faced the biggest fiscal confiscation if he had won, since the British top rate of tax is now effectively higher than every other competitor country. And it is worth bearing in mind that Roger Federer faced a tax bill of about 20 per cent. I am not suggesting that Murray would have won with a lower tax rate, but in the end, at the margin, across the board, I am afraid that high rates of personal taxation are likely to make us less competitive."

> The Age of Enterprise speech to the CBI annual conference, 20 November 2012.

"I don't think that that is necessarily the end of the world. Don't forget that fifteen years ago the entire CBI, British industry, the City, everybody was prophesying that there would be gigantic mutant rats with gooseberry eyes swarming out of the gutters in the sewer to gnaw the last emaciated faces of the remaining British bankers because we didn't go into the Euro. But I want to stress that that is not my preferred option."

> On the possibility of a British EU exit, *The Andrew Marr Show*, December 2012.

"This is possibly the most deluded measure to come from Europe since Diocletian tried to fix the price of groceries across the Roman Empire."

On plans to cap bankers' bonuses, February 28, 2013. Diocletian tried to calm a chaotic empire in AD 301 by imposing maximum prices on common goods, attempting to stop inflation.

"Whoa there, I hope you haven't just spent a happy weekend of pottering about and improving your home, in the way of British families for hundreds of years. Forget about the conservatory, folks. Stuff the new kitchen. You want my advice, you will let it all slide. If you see one of those damp patches appear on the ceiling – about the size and colour of a poppadom – you should just lie back and watch it grow. If the floorboards yawn open, just cover the gap with cardboard. Never mind the state of the downstairs lavatory. A faint aroma of ammonia never hurt anyone. Drip from the ceiling? Shove a bucket under it. I tell you why I offer these household tips: they are the only sensible response to the first policy Ed Miliband has offered the British people.

Rejecting Labour's proposed mansion tax, *Daily Telegraph*, February 17, 2013.

"To understand what has happened in Europe in the last week, we must borrow from the rich and fruity vocabulary of Australian political analysis. Let us suppose you are losing an argument. The facts are overwhelmingly against you, and the more people focus on the reality the worse it is for you and your case. Your best bet in these circumstances is to perform a manoeuvre that a great campaigner describes as 'throwing a dead cat on the table, mate'.

That is because there is one thing that is absolutely certain about throwing a dead cat on the dining room table – and I don't mean that people will be outraged, alarmed, disgusted. That is true, but irrelevant. The key point, says my Australian friend, is that everyone will shout 'Jeez, mate, there's a dead cat on the table!'; in other words they will be talking about the dead cat, the thing you want them to talk about, and they will not be talking about the issue that has been causing you so much grief.

What do the MEPs do, when they behold the pain – the physical suffering – being endured by innocent Greeks? They chuck a dead cat on the table, and have a pop at the bankers in London.

A referendum! The very word is one, as we all know, that causes the Eurocrats to choke on their Douwe Egberts and spray the room with fragments of hysterical Speculoos biscuit. Mon dieu, dio mio, Gott in Himmel, they cry. Anything but democracy! What can they say when this idiot savant continues to blurt the truth about the euro and Italy's inability to deal with its debt? There is nothing to say – nothing to do but to cause a diversion, bash financial services in London, and thank the lord for the 101 uses of a dead cat."

On European plans to cut bankers' bonuses, *Daily Telegraph*, March 3, 2013.

5

MR MAYOR – BORIS IN CITY HALL

"Why would I? Why would I want some beery whip telling me to do this, do that? Why would I want to be told by whips to go and vote at 10pm? Even if I was a secretary of state, why would I want some cabinet committee telling me what I can or can't do? Now I'm feeling guilty about the beery whips. Too late. The only point I was trying to make, perhaps in too colourful a way, is that compared to being mayor of London, most other jobs in politics are not as attractive."

On the suggestion he might return to the Commons.

"The glass gonad."

On City Hall.

"I'm on the, er, upper epidermis of the gonad. Somewhere near the seminal vesical, I expect."

Daily Telegraph interview, June 6, 2008.

"I'm by nature a libertarian, but I thought there was a general freedom that people ought to have to be able to sit on the Tube late at night without having some guy with a six pack of beer leering at them in a threatening way. Thousands of young people were hurling execration at my name. I thought: this is fantastic. It took Margaret Thatcher ten years before she had mobs of urban youth denouncing her."

On banning drink on public transport, *Wall Street Journal*, January 2009.

"I can assure you that we have worked like blazes over the past few days, but one of the joys has been driving around in the care of

Mayor Bloomberg's police detail. It is a very detailed detail. He has no fewer than 30 officers assigned to him, all of them seemingly enormous, charming and good-humoured cops. Such is Mike Bloomberg's Olympian authority that he has not only banned smoking throughout the city, but also issued a fatwa against some forms of margarine. The whole thing makes me feel a bit inadequate. But then I suppose he is the 108th Mayor of New York, and I am only the second Mayor of London... Speaking to the media in Times Square, I am very proud to be surrounded by loads of cameras. Then it turns out they have come for the Belgian winner of the Women's US Open tennis. A tourist takes my picture and then asks, 'Who is that guy?' He's the Mayor of London, says one of my team. 'Oh really,' says the tourist, 'where is he from?'"

On his visit to New York, 2009.

"In the London borough of Walthamstow, there is a cake factory, ladies and gentleman. This cake factory is manufacturing every year £5 million worth of chocolate cake, brownies and dense chocolate puddings to France! That is the kind of ingenuity in London. There's a further twist – how do you think the Walthamstow firm gets more and more cake to pass French lips, and this goes to the heart, the essence, the genius of the London economy, they call it Gü, with an umlaut, so the poor bamboozled French assume that it's Austrian cake."

Speech to the Federation of Small Businesses Annual Dinner, 2009.

"I am pleased that we're replacing 1,000 traffic lights a year, we're beginning the elimination of the bendy buses – it won't be long before the last pair of breeding bendy buses are driven from our streets."

Speech to the Federation of Small Businesses, 12 November 2009.

"There we were on the tarmac at Heathrow as the papal jet prepared to land. The cameras were trained on the night sky. The red carpet was rolled out. The charming Foreign Office people tried for the umpteenth time to remind me where to stand – and all the while my mind was whirring with a single question. It is a problem that goes to the heart of the relationship between church and state. It is a question that will be studied by future generations of students of theology and patristics, because the answer we give – and the answer you give, off the top of your head – is an indication of the balance currently existing between the privileges of spiritual leaders and the egalitarian demands of our temporal world.

Never mind abortion or paedophile priests. As Pope Force One taxied towards us, there was one issue still revolving in my mind at the speed of a Rolls-Royce fan jet. Should the Popemobile be liable for the congestion charge and, if not, why not? Should the Holy Father have to pay £8 to drive through Westminster, like everyone else? Or should that fee be waived, in recognition of his status as the Vicar of Christ on Earth?"

On the Pope's official visit, *Daily Telegraph*,
September 30, 2010.

"Sod it, the sodding mayor had been somewhere else."

On being in the Canadian Rockies during the
2011 London riots, to Michael Cockerell, BBC,
March 25, 2013.

"It was necessary to be, er, pithy in my comments."

"We fought to keep London from lurching back into the grip of a Marxist cabal of taxpayer-funded, Chateauneuf de Pape-swilling tax-minimisers and bendy-bus fetishists... Thank you first for all you did to make sure that we Conservatives won in London this year, and thanks to that intrepid expeditionary force of volunteers from around the country, the busloads from Herefordshire who cross deep along the Ho Chi Minh trail into Hackney where they of course found people's problems really aren't so different after all."

"Go to tech city and see young Londoners devising apps so that teenagers in America can watch movies on their Xbox. Go to Soho and see them doing the special effects for so called Hollywood movies. When they eat cake on the Champs Elysees, they eat cake made in London. When they watch Gangnam Style on their TVs in Korea, they watch it on TV aerials made in London. The Dutch ride bicycles made in London. The Brazilians use mosquito repellent made in London. Every single chocolate Hobnob in the world is made in London. We export everything from badger shaving brushes to ballet shoes. And as I look ahead I am filled with confidence about the capital."

On the potential of the UK economy, Conservative Party Conference, October 2012.

"Holy deadlock! Holy hanging chad, this thing is going to the wire. As things stand, it really does look as though the US presidential election could be a photo-finish. Obama and Romney have spent about a billion each. They have churned the air of countless supermarket car parks and factory canteens with their can-do slogans, and with barely 24 hours until polls open, they are like two spent swimmers that cling to one another and choke their art.

The destiny of the free world could turn this Tuesday evening on whether or not a union-driven busload of Ohio pensioners has some satnav malfunction and gets stuck in a bog on the way to the polls. It's as finely balanced, some say, as a chap walking a tightrope backwards blindfolded across Niagara on one peg-legged foot with the encyclopaedia on his head. A gust of wind either way could make all the difference.

And all you need to create that final gust – that teensy zephyr to tip it one way or the other – is a butterfly flap in some far-flung country.

I know such a country. Each of the candidates is in search of a last-minute game-changer. I have just the thing.

Romney should announce now – just as those febrile Ohioans are making up their mind on that secondary but still important question of whether or not the Republican will bring reassurance around the world – that as soon as he sits down behind that desk in the Oval Office, he will sign the order for all American diplomatic vehicles in London to pay the congestion charge. He will instantly write a cheque for the fines that US vehicles have incurred, now standing at more than £7 million, in the course of about 61,000 infractions since the scheme began. And if he does, Mitt will have my support.

Mind you, I would support Obama if he did the same."

On the 2012 presidential election, *Daily Telegraph*, November 5, 2012. The American Embassy's refusal to pay the congestion charge has been a bone of contention for both Ken Livingstone and Boris Johnson.

"On a day when the sans-culottes appear to have captured the government in Paris and a French minister has been so eccentric as to call for a massive Indian investor to depart from France, I have no hesitation or embarrassment in saying to everyone here, 'venez à Londres, mes amis.'"

Calling for Indian firms to relocate to London in November 2012, after Arnaud Montebourg, an industry minister, reportedly told *Les Echos*, "We don't want Mittal in France any more because they haven't respected France" after the steelmaker closed two blast furnaces in the Florange region.

"London leads the rest of the world in nanotechnology; in biotech; in academic health science, with a growing constellation of power along the Euston Road – now including the Francis Crick Centre aka Europe's largest rat abattoir.

I could take you to Shoreditch, and show you brilliant young men and women in funny-shaped glasses who can do the *Times* upper-fiendish Sudoku in four minutes flat, and who are coming up with apps that will let children in Ohio watch videos on their Playstations, which is good for London in some way that they explained to me."

Speech to the CBI, November 2012.

"I expect Sigmund Freud would have a word or two to say about it, but there is something about the sight of a steam train that seems to turn adult males into bug-eyed adolescents. As for steam trains entering underground tunnels – phwoar!"

On the 150th anniversary of the London Underground, January 14, 2013.

"Hi Nick, it's Boris here from Islington. I just want to ask you when are you going to get all those Government ministers out of their posh limos and onto public transport like everybody else? How can we possibly expect Government to vote for increases in infrastructure spending which we need in this city and upgrading the Tube, which we all need, when they sit in chauffeur-driven limousines – paid for by the taxpayer – rather than getting down on public transport with the rest of us? Nick, get them out of their limos! Boris, over and out."

Boris ambushes Nick Clegg on an LBC radio phone-in, February 6, 2013.

"Great, supine, protoplasmic, invertebrate jellies."

On London Assembly members after they voted against grilling him over planned budget decisions.
February 25, 2013.

6

BORIS AND DAVE – RACE TO THE TOP

"I'm backing David Cameron's campaign purely out of pure, cynical self-interest."

On the 2005 Conservative leadership contest, the *Independent*, October 5, 2005.

"My ambition silicon chip has been programmed to try to scramble up this cursus honorum, this ladder of things, so you do feel a kind of sense you have got to."

Desert Island Discs, October 30, 2005.

"I'm the mayor of London and he's Prime Minister. I'm older than him, I'm considerably heavier. I beat him at tennis the other day, though I think he's better at tennis to tell you the truth."

When asked by Jeremy Paxman how he differed from Cameron, 2011 Conservative Party Conference.

Paxman: "Are there any political differences between you and Cameron?"

Boris: "This is a really good 'when did you stop beating your wife' question, you've cooked it up carefully."

Paxman: "As you well know, people out there are talking all the time about who's going to be the next leader, and they see it as a race between you and George Osborne. Would a Boris leadership be different to a Cameron leadership?"

Boris: "I think my chances of leading the Conservative Party are slightly less good than your chances, Jeremy."

Paxman: "Can we take it then, given your whole-hearted commitment to your role as mayor of London that if you are re-elected there is no possibility of you standing for parliament?"

Boris: "There is not a snowball's chance in Hades."

Paxman: "You mention Dave. Is it true that you've always felt yourself intellectually inferior?"

Boris: "Inferior? No..."

Paxman: "No... This of course goes back to the days when he got a First and you didn't."

Boris: "Ah. Yes."

Paxman: "Does that still rankle a bit?"

Boris: "Well it would if it wasn't in PPE."

To Jeremy Paxman on how he differed from Cameron, 2011 Conservative Party Conference.

Similar attempts to play on the rivalry have been made before, as on *The Andrew Marr Show* in 2009:

Boris: "He got it right up the political agenda in a way that no other politician had done, and I think that the Conservatives are well placed to deliver pragmatic measures that will actually make a difference."

Marr: "We didn't invite you onto this programme to sit there and be nice about David Cameron."

Boris: "I don't know why you invited me onto the programme at all, but I'm delighted to be here."

"I think he was only pretending. I think he knew full well what Magna Carta means. It was a brilliant move in order to show his demotic credentials and that he didn't have Latin bursting out of every orifice."

On David Cameron's performance on the *David Letterman Show*, September 2012.

"My chances of being prime minister are about as good as the chances of finding Elvis on Mars or being reincarnated as an olive."

"Everyone who studies British politics knows my realistic chances of becoming Prime Minister are only slightly better than my chances of being decapitated by a Frisbee, blinded by a champagne cork, locked in a disused fridge or reincarnated as an olive. I'm 47 now; I hear the thrumming roar of young men in a hurry, and young women obviously."

Hay Literary Festival, 3 June 2012

"If ministers are setting out their stall now ... they should save their breath and cool their porridge."

On anyone, Theresa May in particular, who was planning to topple David Cameron, March 2013.

"All politicians in the end are like crazed wasps in a jam jar, each individually convinced that they are going to make it."

On his ambitions, November 2005.

"I think it's a very tough job being prime minister. Obviously, if the ball came loose from the back of a scrum – which it won't – it would be a great, great thing to have a crack at. But it's not going to happen."

To Michael Cockerell, BBC, March 25, 2013.

"If, like the Roman leader Cincinnatus, I were to be called from my plough to serve in that office I wouldn't, of course, say no."

> March 22, 2013, to a schoolchild in Norwood.
> Cincinnatus was a retired Roman statesman and farmer,
> called on to save Rome in 458 BC. In just 16 days, he
> saved Rome from invaders. He then returned to his farm
> and picked up his plough.

"Hypocrisy is at the heart of our national character – without the oil of hypocrisy, the machinery of convention would simply explode."

> *Daily Telegraph*, July 15, 2008.

"How could anyone elect a prat who gets stuck in a zipwire?"

> Dismissing speculation that he could be PM one day,
> referring to his accident in Victoria Park during the
> Olympics, August 2012.

7
POLITICIANS I HAVE KNOWN...

ON MARGARET THATCHER

"There is no need here to rehearse the steps of matricide. Howe pounced, Heseltine did his stuff. After it was all over, my wife, Marina, claimed she came upon me, stumbling down a street in Brussels, tears in my eyes, and claiming that it was as if someone had shot Nanny."

> On Margaret Thatcher's resignation, *Lend Me Your Ears* [2004].

"I was never one of those acnoid Tory boys who had semi-erotic dreams about Margaret Thatcher.

She never visited me at night in her imperial-blue dress and bling and magnificent pineapple-coloured hair. I never imagined her leaning over me and parting her red lips to whisper about monetarism and taming union power. But, even as an apathetic and cynical teenager, I could see that she was doing some tough things."

On the appeal of Lady Thatcher, *Daily Telegraph*,
March 2009.

ON TONY BLAIR

"As snow-jobs go, this beats the Himalayas. He is a mixture of Harry Houdini and a greased piglet. He is barely human in his elusiveness. Nailing Blair is like trying to pin jelly to a wall."

On Tony Blair and the Hutton Report, *Daily Telegraph*,
January 29, 2004.

"His lips twitch upwards, waiting to burst open in a glistening crescent of confidence."

Boris on Tony Blair's smile.

"I forgot that to rely on a train, in Blair's Britain, is to engage in a crapshoot with the devil."

Daily Telegraph, July 3, 2003.

"The Tuscan palazzo of Count Girolamo Strozzi where Tony Blair forged one of New Labour's few hard-edged ideological positions: he was pro-sciutto and anti-pasto."

"I lacked the chameleon skills of Tony Blair, who knows just how to affect a glottal stop and drop an aitch on Richard and Judy."

On his sacking from the Radio 4 programme, *The Week in Westminster*, because he was too posh.

"He persuades his poor lobotomised back-benchers to support invasion of a Third World country on the ground that said country possesses WMD, capable of being fired at us within 45 minutes, and expects them to remain loyal to him when it turns out that (a) Saddam Hussein boasted no WMD more fearful than a tub of superannuated taramasalata, and (b) the CIA had expressly warned the British government that the 45-minute claim was a load of old cobblers. He's lost the plot, people tell me. He's drifting rudderless in the wide Sargasso Sea of New Labour's ideological vacuum."

"A spectre is haunting Europe, my friends. That spectre has a famously toothy grin and an eye of glistering sincerity and an almost diabolical gift of political self-reinvention. Barely two years after he stood down as prime minister, it seems that Tony Blair is about to thrust himself back into our lives. It turns out that he is not content merely to be in charge of brokering peace in the Middle East – which you would have thought was a full-time job for anyone. It isn't enough to potter around the world making speeches about climate change and Africa. He wants more, much more, than to consecrate his remaining days to the promotion of inter-faith dialogue and school sport."

On the prospect of Blair taking the mooted EU presidency, *Daily Telegraph*, October 5, 2009.

ON GORDON BROWN

"He is like some sherry-crazed old dowager who has lost the family silver at roulette, and who now decides to double up by betting the house as well. He is like a drunk who has woken to the most appalling hangover, and who reaches for the whisky bottle to help him dull the pain."

On Brown's response to the 2008 economic crisis, when the top income tax rate was increased to 45p in the pound, *Daily Telegraph*, November 2008.

"Bring it on! My message to Gordon Brown through the *Wall Street Journal* is: You great big, quivering, gelatinous, invertebrate jelly of indecision, you marched your troops to the top of the hill in October of 2007. Show us that you've got enough guts to have an election on June 4. Gordon: Man or Mouse?"

Boris gives a response to rumours of a general election being called, *Wall Street Journal*, January 3, 2009.

"As I write these words, Gordon Brown is still holed up in Downing Street. He is like some illegal settler in the Sinai desert, lashing himself to the radiator, or like David Brent haunting *The Office* in that excruciating episode when he refuses to acknowledge that he has been sacked. Isn't there someone – the Queen's private secretary, the nice policeman on the door of Number 10 – whose job it is to tell him that the game is up?"

On Brown's attempts to stay in power after the 2010 general election, *Daily Telegraph*, May 10, 2010.

"The two men look vaguely similar; they both appear to believe in the efficacy of Grecian 2000; they both favour long and rambling speeches on socialist economic and political theory, with Col Gaddafi's efforts perhaps having a slight edge in logic and coherence."

On Gordon Brown and Colonel Gaddafi, *Daily Telegraph*, February 28, 2011.

"Here was a man, just like the readers of *GQ, Esquire, Loaded* – all the reassurance-craving magazines that have sprouted in the last 10 years – who was endlessly fascinated by the various advantages and disappointments of his own gonads."

On Alan Clark.

"There is one obvious solution, and that is to infect these vast new market economies – as fast as possible – with the British disease. We must spread the sclerosis. We must get the East addicted to our vices. And that is why it might be an idea to ensure that the gospel of Ed Miliband is heard across the planet. You will remember how the Germans brilliantly destabilised Russia in 1917, by sending Lenin in a sealed train from Zurich to the Finland Station in St Petersburg. We could send the human panda to Beijing, in the same spirit of discreet sabotage."

On Ed Miliband's speech at the 2011 Labour party conference, in which the Labour leader promised a break from New Labour's light-touch regulation of financial services.

"Who else is there to emerge with any credit from the smoking wreckage of the Labour campaign? There is one man whose reputation – amazingly – has been burnished by the disaster of the past few weeks; one man who is still sought after by society hostesses; one man whose every silken Voldemortian utterance is still taken down, with reverence, by the political journalists. It is wholly fitting, after the disastrous stewardship of Gordon Brown, that the man best placed to rescue the New Labour project from Cleggmania and reassure the middle classes is the ermine-sporting, eyebrow-arching aristocrat of the party, the grandson of Herbert Morrison, the Deputy Prime Minister, Lord President of the Council, President of the Board of Trade and Lord High Everything Else, Lord Mandelson of Foy and Hartlepool."

On who should succeed Gordon Brown as Labour leader,
Daily Telegraph, May 3, 2010.

"Everybody, not just Tories, should be grateful to the Cleggster, a man who has effectively laid down his political life so that the government of the country can be carried on, and who has endured the most protracted political humiliation since the emperor Valerian was captured by the Persian emperor Shapur, and turned first into a living footstool, and then flayed and used as a rather striking wall hanging."

On Nick Clegg, *Daily Telegraph*, September 24, 2012.

"A bunch of Trotskyist, car-hating, Hugo Chavez-idolising, newt-fancying hypocrites and bendy-bus fetishists."

On Ken Livingstone and his London administration,
Conservative Spring Conference, March 5, 2012.

"There is something unsettling about a man who never touches alcohol, goes to bed at 9 pm, holds Bible-study meetings every morning and who is unable to eat a pretzel without nearly dying. Then there is his command of English. At one point Bush was on the giant screen before us, explaining that his wife Laura believed children should be encouraged to read. 'She wants America to be the most literate nation for every child,' he said, the gears of his brain audibly crunching. One can see what he means, but it's just maddening that, when asked to form a simple declarative sentence on child literacy, the leader of the free world is less articulate than my seven-year-old."

On George W Bush, at the 2004 Republican convention.

"There are all sorts of reasons for hoping that Barack Hussein Obama will be the next president of the United States. He seems highly intelligent. He has an air of courtesy and sincerity. Unlike the current occupant of the White House, he has no difficulty in orally extemporising a series of grammatical English sentences, each containing a main verb."

On Barack Obama, *Daily Telegraph*, October 21, 2008.

"I defy anyone to watch one of those internet anthologies of Bushisms – the gaffes and bloopers of the outgoing president – without a sense of wonderment at his Prescottian battles with the English language. In his gift for surreal improvisation he resembles an unintentional Paul Merton, a linguistic dada-ist, armed with nuclear weapons and a worrying sense that God is on his side. No longer will the White House be inhabited by a man who blissfully jumbles Slovakia and Slovenia, who fears for the fate of the 'Kosovians', or who believes that the secret of Balkan stability is 'to keep good relations with the Grecians', with their lustrous black locks.

We say goodbye to the global strategist whose sunny optimism still persuades him that Japan and America have 'had a peaceful alliance for 150 years' – something of a revelation, one imagines, to the people of Pearl Harbour or Hiroshima – and we say goodbye to the conservative thinker and moralist who simultaneously understands that 'families is where our nation finds hope, where wings take dream', and who yet finds compassion in his heart for the unmarried mother of two. 'I know how hard it is for you to put food on your family,' he told her, and we can all attest to that profound truth, especially when they won't keep still."

On the outgoing George W Bush, *Daily Telegraph*,
January 12, 2009.

"The Jeevesian wearer of cardinal's mauve socks whom Chirac mistakenly allowed to be prime minister."

On Édouard Balladur, a possible successor to Mitterand, in
Lend Me Your Ears [2003].

8

OLYMPIC HERO

"It was a very jammy trick to pull to be mayor during the Olympics."

To Michael Cockerell, BBC, March 25, 2013.

"I say this respectfully to our Chinese hosts, who have excelled so magnificently at ping pong. Ping pong was invented on the dining tables of England, ladies and gentlemen, in the 19th century. It was, and it was called Wiff Waff. And there, I think, you have the essential difference between us and the rest of the world. Other nations, the French looked at the dining table and saw an opportunity to have dinner. We looked at a dining table and saw an opportunity to play wiff waff, and that is why London is the sporting capital of the world, and I say to the world, I say to the Chinese, that ping pong is coming home."

At the handover ceremony in Beijing, August 24, 2008.

"We have a new monument in this city to the indomitability of London. A symbol of resilience to go with Nelson's Column or the dome of St Paul's rising above the smoke of the Blitz. My friends, I give you the Olympic Clock! No sooner had this masterpiece of the Swiss chronometers' art been installed than it unexpectedly packed up. But, with the help of various Swiss chronometers, we got it going again. And then it was attacked by a horde of hooded crusties protesting about something or other, and still that clock ticks on to remind us that nothing and no one is going to stop us in our work of preparing London for the greatest event that has taken place in this city in the last 50 years."

Boris marks one year until the beginning of the Games, in a speech in Trafalgar Square, July 27, 2011.

"As Henry VIII discovered, with at least two of his wives, this is the perfect place to bring an old flame."

On the arrival of the Olympic torch at the Tower of London, July 19, 2012.

"There are some people who are coming from around the world who don't yet know about all the preparations we've done to get London ready over the last seven years. I hear there's a guy called Mitt Romney who wants to know whether we're ready. He wants to know whether we're ready. Are we ready? Are we ready? Yes we are! The venues are ready, the stadium is ready, the aquatics centre is ready, the velodrome is ready, the security is ready, the police are ready, the transport system is ready, and our Team GB athletes are ready aren't they. They're going to win more gold, silver and bronze medals than you'd need to bail out Greece and Spain put together."

Rejecting Mitt Romney's doubts about whether London is ready for the games in a speech to 60,000 people in Hyde Park, July 26, 2012.

"The Geiger counter of Olympo-mania is going to go zoink off the scale."

At the same ceremony.

"Get me a ladder."

On being trapped on a zipwire in Victoria Park, Hackney,
August 1, 2012.

"It got very tight around the groin area."

Ditto.

"That was more painful and frightening than you might think. It was jolly high up and, after you were stuck up there for a while, things began to chafe, and so on and so forth."

To Michael Cockerell, BBC, March 25, 2013.

"And the first [reason to celebrate] is GGGGOLD!!! What a brilliant strategy our team had in those first few nail-biting days – lulling the opposition into a false sense of security. Since my last dispatch, Team GB has amassed an El Dorado of bullion, enough to make up for Gordon Brown's disastrous decision to flog our reserves, enough to bail out the Greeks, and enough to put us – yes, folks, little old Britain – in third place on the medal table. It isn't so long ago that French leader François Hollande was over here, gloating about how France was beating us hollow. Well, M le Président, mettez-ça dans votre pipe et fumez-le! Bien je jamais, eh!

The Games so far are a particular triumph for British women, and for female emancipation in general. It was great to see that female judo competitor from Saudi Arabia – the first in history. She may have got squashed, but Saudi women will never look back. In fact, the whole business is encouraging us all to get in touch with our feminine side. Athletes, spectators, politicians – we are all blubbing like Andy Murray on a bad day. Can you blame us? Go on – let it all out. There, there, feeling better? Blow your nose on this.

We have not only revived the ancient cult of near-nudity in the beach volleyball. The park also boasts a bronze plaque with an ode to the Games in Pindaric Greek."

Daily Telegraph, August 6, 2012.

"In rowing alone, they have delivered our greatest aquatic triumph since Trafalgar."

On Team GB during his GQ 'Man of the Year' acceptance speech, September 4, 2012.

"More than anything I can remember, the Games have moved us and brought us together. Total strangers have been talking to each other on the Tube. It is as though the city has been crop-dusted with serotonin.

The Olympics are proving to be a boost to tattoo parlours. Plenty of people seem to want their thighs inscribed with 'Oylimpics 2012' and other ineradicable mis-spellings.

As I write these words there are semi-naked women playing beach volleyball in the middle of the Horse Guards Parade immortalised by Canaletto. They are glistening like wet otters and the water is plashing off the brims of the spectators' sou'westers. The whole thing is magnificent and bonkers."

Daily Telegraph, September 10, 2012.

"Folks, let's be clear: Mo Farah is as British as a beefeater in the Tower of London. He is as British as a pint of bitter, as British as a bulldog, as British as a wet bank holiday Monday or a bad pun in a *Carry On* film or a hot Cornish pasty on a cold platform at Reading station."

Daily Telegraph, December 2012.

9

BORIS THE CLASSICIST

"Now one thing you can say about the Romans. They certainly were not cowboy plumbers."

On the Pont du Gard, the Roman aqueduct in France.

"If Augustus had any kind of logistical or military problem, his first reaction, I imagine, was to shout, 'Get Agrippa'."

On Augustus's right hand man, Marcus Vipsanius Agrippa.

"Like Shane Warne doing his flipper."

On a Roman statue of Augustus.

"If you were an ancient Athenian politician and you went bald, things were so much easier. You didn't have to worry that the electorate would harp on about it, as they do when confronted by a bald Tory leader, no matter how brilliant. Take the case of Pericles. The Athenian leader was a bit of a slaphead with a dolichocephalic skull; but instead of going around enduring the jeers of the ancient tabloid media, he had a very cool solution. He just wore a hoplite helmet, morning noon and night."

On bald Tory leaders, *Daily Telegraph*, July 8, 2004.

"You've got to realise they would have done it. They would have gone right ahead and swept another priceless heirloom from the mantelpiece of history. They were revving up their bulldozers, ready to roar into the ancient and irreplaceable ecosystem. Another great tree would have been felled in the forest of knowledge, and the owl of Minerva would have fled in terror from her roost. Had it not been for a few romantic reactionaries, then the technicians who run our reductionist system of education – with the complaisance of the Labour government – would by now be halfway to the demolition of the Ancient History A-level.

When a new Dark Age falls, it is not always to the sound of Viking battle cries and the tinkling of church windows. Sometimes it is the very governments themselves that go mad, and start disembowelling their own culture.

The real trouble is that our rulers are Puritans; what I mean by Puritans is that they cannot see the beauty and point of an academic discipline unless it adds, in some crashingly obvious way, to the Gross Domestic Product of UK Plc. They are Puritans in the sense that they exalt WORK with all the mania of 1930s Soviet agitprop extolling the virtues of *trud*, with meat-forearmed, hammer-wielding women rolling up their sleeves and preparing to join the men at the lathe.

Every skill and every pursuit and every practical effort or undertaking seems to aim at some good, says old Aristotle, my all-time hero, and that goal is happiness – not Gordon's wretched *trud*. In his worship of work, and his Marxist obsession with money, Gordon Brown continually mistakes the means for the end. He does not understand that an educational system can be a eudaemonic triumph even if it encourages disciplines that add not a penny to national output."

On the threat to Ancient History A-Level, the *Spectator*, May 23, 2007.

During his first mayoral electoral campaign in 2008, Boris compared the press to a "ravening Hyrcanian tiger deprived of its mortal prey". The Hyrcanian tiger, now extinct, lived in Hyrcania – an ancient kingdom in what is now Golestan, Mazandaran, Gilan and part of Turkmenistan.

Then, after his victory in May 2008, Boris said that political success hadn't changed him, that there was no "Arian controversy about the old Boris and the new".

Arian is derived from Arius (256 AD-336 AD), a priest from Alexandria, Egypt. Arius was at the heart of the debate in the 3rd and 4th century as to whether Christ was homoousian (from the Greek homoios, meaning same, and ousia, meaning essence or being) with the Father – that is, they are of the same substance and are equally God; or whether he was homoiousios (Greek for "of like substance") with the Father and God.

The difference between the two words was tiny, just one "i" or iota, as they are called in

Greek; thus the expression, there isn't an iota of difference – meaning a minuscule difference.

"There are times when a minister says something so maddening, so death-defyingly stupid, that I am glad not to be in the same room in case I should reach out, grab his tie, and end what is left of my political career with one almighty head-butt.

Such were my feelings on reading Mr Ed Balls on the subject of teaching Latin in schools. Speaking on the radio, Spheroids dismissed the idea that Latin could inspire or motivate pupils. Head teachers often took him to see the benefits of dance, or technology, or sport, said this inter-galactic ass, and continued:

"No one has ever taken me to a Latin lesson to make the same point. Very few parents are pushing for it, very few pupils want to study it."

It is nothing short of a disaster that this man is still nominally in charge of education, science, scholarship and learning in this country.

Latin and Greek are great intellectual disciplines, forcing young minds to think in a logical and analytical way. They allow you to surprise your family and delight your friends by deciphering inscriptions.

They are also a giant universal spanner for other languages. Suppose your kid scrapes her knee on holiday in Italy. You are much more likely to administer the right first aid if you know that caldo means hot rather than cold – as you will, if you know Latin. Suppose you are captured by cannibals in the Mato Grosso, and you find a scrap of Portuguese newspaper in your hut revealing that there is about to be an eclipse; and suppose that by successfully prophesying this event you convince your captors that you are a god and secure your release – I reckon you would be thankful for your Latin, eh?"

Daily Telegraph, March 15, 2010.

"Horace sometimes reads like Melanie Phillips of the *Daily Mail* after a particularly difficult Tube ride. 'Young girls think of sex to the tips of their tender fingers!' 'Is this the race that conquered Antiochus and Hannibal?' asks Simon Heffer. 'I tell you what,' says Peter Hitchens in a provocative personal view, 'Roman wives these days are having it off with Spanish sea captains and travelling salesmen.'"

The Spectator, September 10, 2005.

"Behold this new Olympic torch, the flames
That first blazed forth at Greece's early dawn:
Now give a rousing welcome to these Games,
on London's riverbanks reborn."

Pindaric Ode, composed by Oxford don, Armand
D'Angour, recited by Boris at the Royal Opera House,
July 23, 2012.

10

ON WINE, WOMEN, SONG – AND BICYCLES

"There is one measurement I hesitate to mention, since the last time I did, I am told, the wife of the editor of *The Economist* cancelled her subscription to the *Daily Telegraph* in protest at my crass sexism. It is what is called the Tottometer, the Geiger counter that detects good-looking women. In 1997, I reported these were to be found in numbers at the Labour conference.

Now – and this is not merely my own opinion – the Tories are fighting back in a big way."

The Spectator, February 10, 2001.

"I've got my fingers in several dykes."

Conservative Conference, October 6, 2004.

"I think it'd be disgraceful if a chap wasn't allowed to have a bit of fun in Las Vegas. The real scandal would be if you went all the way to Las Vegas and you didn't misbehave in some trivial way."

Boris supports Prince Harry, BBC news, August 2012.

"A bit like a nymph descending from Parnassus or Olympus."

Boris recalls Ulrika Jonsson teaching him to disco dance.

"I can't remember what my line on drugs is. What's my line on drugs?"

Campaigning for the 2005 general election.

"I think I was given cocaine once but I sneezed so it didn't go up my nose. In fact, it may have been icing sugar."

Evening Standard, October 17, 2005.

"I seemed to be averaging a speed of X and then the M3 opened up before me, a long quiet Bonneville flat stretch, and I am afraid it was as though the whole county of Hampshire was lying back and opening her well-bred legs, to be ravished by the Italian stallion."

On driving a Ferrari, GQ, 2007.

"We seek cities because there are a greater range of girls at the bar of reproductive choice. Number one. Number two is that there are better outcomes for health and wealth. And now we care more about the environment, and cities are better for the environment. But above all, talented people seek cities for fame. They can't get famous in the fucking village."

New York Magazine, June 17, 2012.

"Such is my colossal vanity that I have no intention of trying to forbid you." Boris agrees to allow Andrew Gimson write a biography of him. He later got cold feet:

"If it's a pisstake that's ok. Anything that purported to tell the truth really would be intolerable."

"In the words of Sir Arthur Conan Doyle, my life is like the giant rat of Sumatra, a story for which the world is not yet prepared."

"Couldn't I pay you not to write it?" to Andrew Gimson, his biographer, when he realised salacious details of his private life would be included.

On his biography, Andrew Gimson's *Boris* [2006]

ON BICYCLES, AND OTHER VEHICLES

"Nor do I propose to defend the right to talk on a mobile while driving a car, though I don't believe that is necessarily any more dangerous than the many other risky things that people do with their free hands while driving – nose-picking, reading the paper, studying the A–Z, beating the children, and so on."

Daily Telegraph, August 1, 2002.

"It was a dark and rainy night and I was cycling innocently home at about the speed of an elderly French onion seller, when – pok – something hit me on the side of the helmet. I heard a shout of laughter to my right, and a cry of 'You ------!', and a car sped off up Shaftesbury Avenue. As anyone would in my position, I saw red. I put my foot down, and pedalled so hard that I was able to keep the weaving rump of the car in my sights, and I noted that it was some kind of souped-up Astra, licence plate M★58 H★3.

Soon the bike had beaten the car, as it always does. As they waited at the next set of lights, I pounded on the window. 'Open up!' I cried. There were three kids inside, and I could see the culprit goggling up at me with appalled recognition. They lurched off again in the hope of escape, but of course I had them at the next lights.

'Open up now,' I yelled, 'because you aren't going to get away with it, M★58 H★3! I am the mayor!'

By this time they were starting to look a bit unnerved, and the window came down.

'I know you is the mayor,' said the driver, 'and it was a accident.'

'Pull over!' I commanded. Eventually they pulled over in a street running up towards the British Museum.

'Do you want me to get out?' said the culprit, who obviously had some experience of being flagged down by the law.

'Er, yes,' I said, noticing that it was pretty quiet around there. 'Right!' I said, when we were all assembled. 'Why did you throw something at my head?'

'Please, Mr Boris sir, this wasn't meant to happen.'

'We know you is the mayor, man.'

'We gotta lot of respect for the things you are doing.'

'Hmm,' I said, momentarily wondering where I was going with all this.

'Whose car is this?' I demanded.

'It's my uncle's. We are going back to Clapton after a day trip.'

'Right,' I said. 'And what is your name?'

'My name is Derron.'

'And what is yours?'

'My name is Erron.'

I didn't bother to ask the third chap, having by

now more or less run out of ideas, except for a general desire to stop them doing it again.

'Look, just don't throw things – er – at people's heads, OK.'"

Daily Telegraph, May 30, 2010.

Michael Parkinson: "I just wondered about things that bothered you about Britain that you wanted to bin."

Boris Johnson: "People who shout at me on bicycles. Sorry, people who shout at me when I am on a bicycle. People do shout at me when they are also on bicycles."

Parkinson: "What prompted this business about people shouting at you on a bicycle, there's a story about this isn't there?"

Johnson: "Yes, and I'm trying to remember what it is."

(LATER)

Johnson: "I was cycling, and I was talking on my mobile phone whilst cycling. I was no risk to anybody else, and barely any risk to myself because I was hugging the shore, hugging the pavement, hugging the curb like a ship in the ancient world hugging the coast line, and I was going very very slowly, and a woman overtook me and said 'Get off your phone!' She then said it was illegal to talk on your mobile phone whilst riding a bicycle, and I was able to tell her that not only was it perfectly legal but that insofar as I had anything to do with the promulgation of the laws in respect to riding a bike and talking on your phone, I would make it my work in Parliament to prevent such a law being enacted, and we had a lively exchange of views. I think in retrospect that she wasn't entirely wrong. She then shopped me. She grassed me up. She dobbed me in to the readers of the *Daily Telegraph*."

To Michael Parkinson, BBC, April 22, 2008.

"Every so often I find a new hero. I read in the papers of some individual who is managing to swim against the glutinous tide of political correctness.

In this age of air-bagged, mollycoddled, infantilised over-regulation it can make my spirits soar to discover that out there in the maquis of modern Britain there is still some freedom fighter who is putting up resistance against the encroachments of the state; and when I read of their struggle I find myself wanting to stand on my chair and cheer, or perhaps to strike a City Hall medal in their honour.

Such were my feelings yesterday morning when I read of my new hero, or heroes, to be precise. We are talking of a married couple from Dulwich, south London, by the name of Oliver and Gillian Schonrock. I have not been able to contact this illustrious pair – since it didn't seem fair to phone them up on a Sunday – but if the papers are right, they deserve the thanks of us all. They have taken the sword of common sense to the great bloated encephalopathic sacred cow of elf and safety. And for this effrontery they are, of course, being persecuted by the authorities.

What do they want? They want their children, aged eight and five, to have the right to walk or cycle one mile to school."

Daily Telegraph, July 5, 2010.

"Just as I will never vote to ban hunting, so I will never vote to abolish the freeborn Englishman's time-hallowed and immemorial custom, dating back as far as 1990 or so, of cycling while talking on a mobile."

"In 1904, 20 per cent of journeys were made by bicycle in London. I want to see a figure like that again. If you can't turn the clock back to 1904, what's the point of being a Conservative?"

Said during the launch of the Barclays bicycle hire scheme, July 30, 2010.

"It's a very good way for a conservative to nuke his opponents. People are just sort of flummoxed when you turn out to be a militant cyclist. They associate that with whippet-legged, dreadlocked anarchists."

On bicycling, *New York* magazine, June 17, 2012.

"The other night we were filling in time at Istanbul airport, and I was watching an official dart around on one of those new Segway gizmos. Have you seen one? They are extraordinary. It was as though his feet had grown wheels. This way and that he sheepdogged the passengers, twisting and curvetting and generally running rings round them like some Spanish midfielder.

'What a poser!' I exclaimed. 'He's just showing

off. He doesn't need that thing at all.' And then he pushed down the stick and he shot off into the distance like Usain Bolt – and we understood why he was equipped with electric feet.

There is a scene in *From Russia With Love* when James Bond arrives at what was Yesilkoy airport – with only one terminal, looking like a small whitewashed suburban bungalow, an inferior version of Biggin Hill. Those days are gone, my friends. Today's Ataturk International is colossal.

It is more colossal than an American shopping mall, and that is saying something. Gleaming marble concourses dwindle into the distance, hedged around by luscious watch and chocolate shops, and that's why you need a Segway to get around. As I watched that Turkish official zooming off through the crowds, I had the perfect image of the scale, the dynamism and the technological optimism of the Turkish economy."

Daily Telegraph, August 2, 2010.

"I was cycling through central London the other day when my heart lurched. There it was – in its natural habitat. I felt the surge of excitement that I imagine you must get on safari, when after days of scanning the veld you finally see a representative of some species of charismatic megafauna. I could tell instantly what it was: I recognised the noble curve of the brow, like a bowler hat or an African elephant."

Boris on the new Routemaster bus.

"Pssht, I said to Barry from the High Commission. Look, there, I pointed. There it was, slap bang in the middle of the road. It was a giant cat – as black as Bagheera from The Jungle Book, and if anything a bit bigger. We'd only been in India for about half an hour, and we'd already seen kites circling in the blood-red sun of dawn. We'd seen dewlapped cows grazing on patches of grass by the expressways, and elephants waiting for their mahouts to finish their ablutions in the fields. But this was something else.

We drew nearer. Still it didn't move. 'Are you sure it is?' I asked Barry. He leaned over and put the question to the driver. 'Is that a Jaguar?' 'Yes, sir, it is a Jaguar.'

My friends, it was indeed. Within a few miles of Indira Gandhi Airport, we had found a genuine British Jaguar, waiting at the traffic lights. It was designed at Whitley near Coventry and at Gaydon near Warwick, and assembled into the mighty black beast before us by the workforce of Castle Bromwich near Birmingham. Here, in one of the biggest and fastest-growing markets in the world, I am proud to say that we had found evidence of market penetration by one of this country's proudest motoring marques."

Daily Telegraph, November 27, 2012.

11

BORIS THE CULTURE VULTURE

"I don't see why people are so snooty about Channel 5. It has some respectable documentaries about the Second World War. It also devotes considerable airtime to investigations into lap dancing, and other related and vital subjects."

On television, *Daily Telegraph*, March 14, 2002.

"Treachery, thy name is Edmonds. After decades in which his hairy chops have been clamped about the hind teat of the BBC, Noel Edmonds has announced that he will not pay the licence fee, and I can imagine that some people will declare him a hero.

Never mind that he has spent much of his adult life wallowing in the golden Pactolus of BBC light entertainment; no matter that all his grand homes were funded with the proceeds of characters such as Mr Blobby, which the BBC paid him to inflict upon the nation."

On Noel Edmonds's demand that the licence fee be scrapped, *Daily Telegraph*, September 16, 2008.

"My speaking style was criticized by no less an authority than Arnold Schwarzenegger. It was a low moment, my friends, to have my rhetorical skills denounced by a monosyllabic Austrian cyborg."

On his cameo appearance on *EastEnders*, to Conservative Conference, September 28, 2008.

ON GOD AND MAMMON

"When is Little Britain going to do a sketch, starring Matt Lucas as one of the virgins? Islam will only be truly acculturated to our way of life when you can expect a Bradford audience to roll in the aisles at Monty Python's Life of Mohammed."

"Some readers will no doubt say that a devil is inside me; and though my faith is a bit like Magic FM in the Chilterns, in that the signal comes and goes, I can only hope that isn't so."

Daily Telegraph, March 4, 2004.

"It's chicken feed. I think that frankly there is no reason at all why I should not, on a Sunday morning, before I do whatever else I need to do on a Sunday morning, should not knock off an article."

Boris on his £250,000 salary for his *Telegraph* columns, July 2009.

"A good dry run for the Olympics."

On the wedding of Prince William and Kate Middleton.

BORIS THE JOCK

"At the end of a game of rugby, you sit in the changing room with the relief of one who has just survived being beaten up by the secret police. Your ears ring, your breath comes in gasps, you can hardly focus your eyes on the splodges of mud on the floor. There is absolutely no reason for you to go off and get involved in gang violence because frankly that is what you have been doing for the last couple of hours."

Backing the Hitz programme for expanding rugby in inner city London, *Daily Telegraph*, May 29, 2011.

"As mayor of the host city I am proud to tell you that it was here in London in 1871 that a group of burly moustachioed and mildly inebriated Victorians met at a pub in Cockspur Street called the Pall Mall Restaurant and decided that they had had enough of the namby-pamby, pussy-footing around of the spheroid fetishists of association football, and that it was time to codify a game that more closely resembled unarmed combat – where it was a mark of honour to have your nose spread artistically spread across your left cheek and your ear like a cauliflower, and where you would be actively congratulated and not penalised if you deliberately set out to knock over your opponent in the tackle. The result was Rugby Union, the peerless game of the elliptical ball."

Opening the draw for the group stages of the 2015 Rugby World Cup that will be held in England, December 6, 2012.

"Look, I'm a rugby player really, and I knew I was going to get to him, and when he was about two yards away I just put my head down. There was no malice. I was going for the ball with my head, which I understand is a legitimate move in soccer."

Defending his "tackle" on former Germany midfielder Maurizio Gaudino during a charity football match in May 2006.

"We either unleash a full-hearted attack on the nannying, mollycoddling, Harriet Harperson hopelessness of our times, or else too many of our children will grow up fat, unhappy, or violent; we will never win Wimbledon, and football will remain a game in which, in Gary Lineker's immortal words, 22 men run around for 90 minutes and then the Germans win."

Daily Telegraph, July 1, 2008.

"There is a reason why Germany have succeeded in getting through to the quarter-finals since 1938 and why England have so often failed. I had an insight, an omen, yesterday morning. I got up early to play tennis, at a municipal court. It is a lovely place, an oasis of green, in a densely populated area not far from London; and since I had failed to book I fully expected to be kicked off by 8am. Well, by 9am the courts were still deserted and we played blissfully on. It wasn't until almost 10am – on one of the most glorious days of the year, a day when the whole of nature seems to shout that it's time for tennis – that we were joined on the courts. A nice middle-aged couple turned up and began patting it to each other, and I thought, by heaven, what is wrong with us? Where is the get-up-and-go of our kids?

If this was Germany, they would have been out bagging the courts since dawn! Somewhere along the line the nation that invented or codified virtually every sport seems to have lost its lust for competitive games. I don't want to exaggerate this. We did amazingly at the 2008 Olympics, and we have recently beaten Australia at rugby. But in our game, the world game, we should be doing so much better.

I am sure the problem is partly to do with all those foreign players in the Premiership, but it's more fundamental than that. We are still paying the price of an educational establishment that developed an aversion to competitive games and an obsession with bureaucracy and elf and safety that made it hard for the voluntary sector to fill the gap.

But let's look on the bright side. We have a new government that should be able to change that, and at least it didn't go to penalties."

On England crashing out of the 2010 World Cup at the hands of the Germans, *Daily Telegraph*, June 28, 2010.

"Some time before the end of August I will grab a week's leave, like a half-starved sea lion snatching an airborne mackerel, and whatever happens that leave will not be taken in some boarding house in Eastbourne.

It will not take place in Cornwall or Scotland or the Norfolk broads.

I say stuff Skegness. I say bugger Bognor.

I consider to my patriotic duty to find a destination as sunny and foreign as possible, so that I can push some cash towards hard-pressed UK travel agents, and so that we can minimise, on compassionate grounds, the number of British citizens exposed to the sight of my swimming trunks."

Daily Telegraph, July 22, 2008.

"All other buildings look like they've been put on earth by people, but the Shard is like something that is prodding up. Prodding up through the frail integuments of our planet, like an intergalactic spear. It's like the tip of a cocktail stick emerging through the skin of a colossal pickled onion."

Opening the observation deck of the Shard, the tallest building in western Europe, February 1, 2013.

"More hot air than the wind section of the London Philharmonic."

Boris's first press release as Shadow Arts Minister on Labour's plans for music in schools, 2004.

"I stood behind Posh in a ski queue and saw the tattoos on her bum. I like her."

> On Victoria Beckham, in an interview with Piers
> Morgan in *GQ*.

"Suppose you are a Martian anthropologist. You crash-land in Britain. You pick up a paper and you read of the rage of the natives who have been hoodwinked into eating horse meat in their lasagne. You read of the ministerial attempts to console the grief-stricken public, the disquiet of Number 10 that this 'distasteful' item should creep on to the national menu. You note the general hysteria. You then take a train to a Paris restaurant, and with your DNA probe-cum-Biro you identify the dark, sweet, gamey slab of steaming meat before you.

Yes, you are being invited to tuck in to the very same equine quadruped that has been tearfully rejected by the British public.

Amazing! Here are two nations, with roughly the same level of civilisation, with a densely interwoven history, a cognate language – but who have entered the internet age with radically different ideas about eating humanity's eternal helpmeet. In fact, the further you whizz around the world, the more unusual the British scruple seems to be. From Mexico to Kazakhstan, you find people eating horse flesh – and the Chinese manage to chomp through an astonishing 1.7 million gee-gees every year.

You feel like Captain Cook, when he first came across the phenomenon among the South Sea Islanders."

On the horsemeat scandal, *Daily Telegraph*, February 11, 2013.

"A man's got to know his limitations, says Clint Eastwood in *Magnum Force*, although, for most of us, the struggle with reality is very hard. It is only now, after half a lifetime of consistent failure, that I am on the verge of recognising that I was not born to be a musician.

I suppose I should have seen the signs at the age of eight, when my sister and I attended Princess Road Primary School, Camden. Like most of our generation, we were issued with Dolmetsch descant recorders. She could play a tune called 'Hurry, Hurry, Down the Street', while my own instrument emitted nothing but a shrill peep and a worrying quantity of warm spit.

The recorder, I decided, was a girly instrument so, by the age of 11, I was grappling with the trombone – just the job to express my musical personality, I thought; and yet if anything, the trombone seemed less easy to control than the recorder.

Sometimes, you could blow so hard into the mouthpiece that you saw stars and nothing would come out except a soft windy afflatus. Sometimes, it would give vent to a horrible parp. There was simply no predicting it.

After a while, I laid the trombone aside, consoling myself with the thought that it was all a matter of practice, and it was not until I was 17 that I decided to make my final assault on the summit of Parnassus. By this stage, I was smarting from being fired from a rock band on the not unreasonable grounds that I was the only would-be bass guitarist in history who could not play the opening bars of 'Smoke on the Water'. I knew that this had been a potentially life-changing moment. I knew it could mark the death of my hopes to be the Mick Jagger of my generation. So I decided to acquire the fundamentals. I took up the piano.

After months of brow-beading effort, in which I drove my housemaster half-insane by practising next to his study (and substantially delaying his otherwise brilliant translation of Homer), I was ready to take grade one. I had the scales off pat, more or less. With a bit of effort I could read the notes. The tricky bit was the actual tune, which was a nice little number by Bach called 'Lord, Do With Me What Thou Will'.

Confident young plonker though I was, I remember my heart pounding with nerves as I began, and I remember my horror as the Lord began to do what he wanted with my fingers.

After three minutes, I had so massacred Bach that I became one of the first pupils in years to fail grade one piano; and still I persevered, in spite of the gentle whispering campaign mounted by my piano teacher to persuade me to give up.

To this day, if you are so unlucky as to pass our house on a Saturday afternoon, you will hear strange clanking versions of 'On Top Of Old Smokey' and 'When The Saints Go Marching In', left-hand and right-hand version. Because there is still part of me that believes that with just a little more effort, and a little more practice, I could unlock the pent-up Mozart within; and yet there is another part of me that has come to the reluctant conclusion that I am useless."

On learning music, *Daily Telegraph*, January 20, 2009.

"As soon as *Fifty Shades* took off, the DIY shops reported a troubling surge in the demand for rope, of a kind that could be used to strap your partner to the bed without doing unnecessary damage to her wrists. Some couples said that their relationships had been saved. In other cases, it was said, there were chaps who felt a bit unmanned by the sudden feminine demand for reef-knots and general masterfulness."

On *Fifty Shades of Grey*, *Daily Telegraph*,
December 23, 2012.

"Can there be a household that will not attempt to brighten up a long family binge by going to *YouTube* and turning up the volume on the laptop? Soon the whole family is pretending to flick the reins, while the knees go up and down like pistons and overweight uncles snap their hamstrings. I have read of at least one sad death caused by the strain of performing the absurd pony-like prancing, and feel sure that others will succumb in the days ahead.

Let's be frank, I think most of us had only a very hazy notion of Korea before Psy appeared before us. We had heard of a land of kimchi and roast dog, where giant chaebols produced excellent cars and machine tools. We had no idea about a district called Gangnam, where the women drive a Mercedes-Benz and take group exercise by waving their bums on the banks of the river.

On Gangnam Style, *Daily Telegraph*, December 23, 2012.

"At the risk of sounding like a character from Enid Blyton, there is absolutely nothing to beat camping. I love the exultation you get when you rise from your groundmat and all the aches melt away from your body as you realise the night is over at last. Then follows the sizzle of bacon and the hands wrapped around the mug of tea, and the first peep of sun over mountains or the mist rising off a river; and all the time that wonderful sense that you are the first to be up, that the world is snoozing, and that you have defied nature and survived a night in your own habitation – no matter how rudimentary.

I have camped everywhere from the drizzle of Salisbury Plain to the Serengeti to the beaches of California. I have bivouacked on cardboard outside the Gare du Nord in Paris. I have dossed down on my towel in Spain, and I once accidentally pitched my tent late at night in the middle of a roundabout in downtown Canberra, and woke to found my hands had been so badly bitten by bugs that they swelled like blown up washing-up gloves; and yet I would do it again tomorrow."

Boris is reminded of the joys of camping by the Occupy movement, *Daily Telegraph*, January 23, 2012.

ON FOOD

"My policy on cake is pro having it and pro eating it."

"If I was in charge, I would get rid of Jamie Oliver and tell people to eat what they like."

On Jamie Oliver's healthy eating campaign at the Conservative party conference in 2006. He later described the chef as a "national saint".

"It is one thing to show solidarity with the Scots by eating porridge for breakfast. But can you really face it on its own? Surely the thing is to add brown sugar or — better still — whorls of golden syrup. If you are like me, you take a childish pleasure in watching as it falls from the spoon, a glistening shaft of solid tawny sunlight."

"There comes a time when the Brits can be pushed around no more. We may have sold Rolls-Royce to the Germans. We may have lost Land Rover to the Indians. We have yielded to the French more control of our energy and water supplies than ever envisaged in the wildest fantasies of Bonaparte. But when it comes to protecting our chocolate – the taste of British childhood – then we turn and fight.

We are talking here of Cadbury's Dairy Milk, the king of chocolate. In fact, I don't mind if I am thrown into Pseuds' Corner for saying this, but a block of it strikes me as approaching the Platonic form of the chocolate bar. It is what chocolate is fundamentally intended to look like and taste like. Ever since the Aztecs first worshipped the cocoa bean, mankind has experimented with various ratios of solids, fats, sugar and milk, and Cadbury has got it right.

How many millions of children have woken on a cold Christmas morning to find that reassuring oblong bulking out their stocking? The texture is hard and dense, but not brittle like some of the fancier Swiss brands. When you bite into a big bar of Dairy Milk, you have to flex your jaws like a weapon dog, and when you chomp down you not only have the ambrosial sweetness of the choc; the rugged geometry of the segments helps to emphasise that you are eating something pretty substantial."

Daily Telegraph, December 7, 2009.

"There is a contradiction in Conservative thinking, a mixture a bit like a Cadbury Creme Egg. There is the surface toughness of free-market ideology, the hard necessity of exposure to international competition. Then beneath that is the gooey confusion of a general desire to protect old national institutions, and to honour icons of British culture, and to preserve time-honoured businesses and their dependants.

Which should a Conservative prefer? The hard bit or the soft bit? The reality is that, as with a Creme Egg, you can't have the one without the other."

Daily Telegraph, December 7, 2009.

"On the great questions of pregnancy and birth, there are many details hidden from me. One thing, however, I know. If you happen to be nine months' pregnant, and wondering when junior will make an appearance, I know what to do. If you have one of those babies that seems to prefer the womb to the terrors of the world, I have an infallible solution.

You go to Legoland. To be exact, you go to those deceptively simple whirly teacup things, and you subject the human body to the most extraordinary stresses and shears. Your teacup rotates in one direction. The tea tray spins the other way. After barely a minute of this I guarantee that – pop – you will have the makings of an expensive event.

It is in memory of this breakthrough in obstetrics that, every year, we go to the Windsor-based theme park, built to celebrate those little plastic cuboids that are so painful to tread on in bare feet.

Rain or shine, we always have a lovely time. The great thing about Legoland is that you are outdoors for the whole day and, at the end, you have that nice, stretched, slightly sunburnt feeling, as if you have played a game of cricket.

Every year we look, with enormous satisfaction, at the Lego Grand Place, Lego San Gimignano, Lego Scottish petrol station and all the million and one other tricks you can do with an irritatingly pointy plastic brick."

On Legoland, *Daily Telegraph*, July 29, 2004.

12
OTHER PEOPLE ON BORIS

"An Oxford-educated classics major playing a buffoonishly triumphant super-twit role he's written for himself."

Carl Swanson, *New York* Magazine.

"People always ask me the same question, they say, 'Is Boris a very clever man pretending to be an idiot?' And I always say, 'No.'"

Ian Hislop.

"My own prediction is that Johnson will age into becoming that great character actor Miles Malleson, portraying an elder statesman giving Greek lessons from a deckchair in his nudist club."

Roger Lewis, reviewing Andrew Gimson's biography, 2006.

"His trick has been to play the self-deprecating buffoon while simultaneously making it clear that he is very funny, and not quite as daft as he makes out."

Andrew Sparrow, former *Telegraph* colleague.

"A man blessed with high intelligence and great abilities has, through moral failure and self-indulgence, now largely ceased to be taken seriously in public life."

Simon Heffer, Boris's former *Telegraph* colleague, 2006.

"Boris is the right man to lead us back into the 17th century!"

Paul Merton.

"He is fumbling all over the place!"

Governor of California Arnold Schwarzenegger during a video conference with Boris, October 3, 2007.

"If the day ever comes that Boris Johnson becomes tenant of Downing Street, I shall be among those packing my bags for a new life in Buenos Aires or suchlike, because it means that Britain has abandoned its last pretensions to being a serious country."

Max Hastings, Boris's former editor at the *Telegraph*.

"The selection of Boris Johnson, the *Spectator* editor, as the Tory candidate for Michael Heseltine's Henley constituency, confirms the Tory Party's increasing weakness for celbrity personalities over the dreary exigencies of politics. Johnson, for all his gifts, is unlikely to grace any future Tory cabinet. Indeed, he is not known for his excessive interest in serious policy matters, and it is hard to see him grubbing away at administrative detail as an obscure, hardworking junior minister for social security. To maintain his funny man reputation he will no doubt find himself refining his Bertie Wooster interpretation to the point where theimpersonation becomes the man."

Max Hastings, then editor of the *Evening Standard*, 2000.

"Boris Johnson is without doubt the very worst putative politician I've ever seen in action. He is utterly, chronically useless – and I can't think of a higher compliment."

A.A. Gill on Boris's parliamentary bid for Henley, the *Sunday Times*, 2001.

"Boris is not Prime Minister material. The public want a PM who looks like one. They don't want him to resemble a dishevelled buffoon. Let's end the silly speculation. Boris is the John Prescott of the Tory party."

Philip Davies, Conservative MP for Shipley.

"Mr Johnson's political beliefs are more interesting today than they were in 2001 when he became MP for Henley, a corner of Oxfordshire where the conundrum over whether or not to take off jacket and tie in hot weather counts as a social problem; or in 2008 when he became mayor of London, where his power is mostly limited to transport and policing. The difficulty here is not that Mr Johnson has been coy about what he thinks, but that in 25 years as a journalist and frequent public speaker he has collected so many enthusiasms. It is also easy to confuse a conviction with what is merely a good set-up for a joke."

Bagehot, *Economist*, August 4, 2012

"With amazing symmetry, the Right seems to have found in Boris Johnson a Tory maverick equivalent of his Labour maverick predecessor as mayor. There's something about London – indefinable but you can feel, almost touch it – that makes an eccentric individualist with a touch of roguishness, a touch of the joker and a touch of genius, the best and perhaps only type of candidate that feels right. He doesn't so much have to do, as to be."

Matthew Parris, the *Times*.

"Cleverer (of course) than he pretends, somewhat less doggedly amiable than he pretends, as learned as he seems, not always as confident as he seems, more easily depressed than he appears, he has a real passion for wronged individuals and the overlooked. He would have been a brave defender of Dreyfus. He can be a good friend in need. However, he sometimes finds arguments in principle, in the abstract, or about ideology rather tiresome. Personally energetic, he can be philosophically lazy."

Matthew Parris.

"Most politicians, as far as I can work out, are pretty incompetent, and then have a veneer of competence. You do seem to do it the other way round."

Jeremy Clarkson, interviewing Boris on *Top Gear*.

"It seems to be the fate of Conservative prime ministers to be stalked by flamboyantly ambitious blonds with connections to Henley, wild hair and untamed rhetoric. In the case of Margaret Thatcher, it was Michael Heseltine, her nemesis but not her successor. For David Cameron, the predator is Boris Johnson, who pulsates with the urge to do both."

Andrew Rawnsley, the *Observer*.

"Watching London's Mayor crank himself from comatose to Maximum Boris at eight in the morning is quite a sight. It's like witnessing a volcano erupt: first a few wisps of smoke, then the first plumes of fire spring forth. Finally there is the full eruption: an explosion of pungent articulation, semi-formed thoughts, off-hand ripostes disguised as misdirection, and florid words that haven't been aired since the first Queen Elizabeth."

Elliot Wilson, GQ.

"It is odd that people still resist him. An ever-shrinking but stubbornly disbelieving core still thinks he is:

1) Not real – not cuddly, but, in fact, remote, cold, impersonal.
2) A buffoon – a show-off and dangerously ridiculous figure.

3) A lazy sod – a disorganised rogue who doesn't put in the hours.
4) Without beliefs or principles – he'll say or do anything to please the crowd.
5) A toff – a class joke on a new Britain.

Most politicians, in the face of such resistance and 'negatives', re-calibrate and reposition. But Boris is not so much a politician – with a quasi-scientific approach to the management of popular opinion – but a seducer. In the playbook of seduction, he amps it up, continues coming, keeps playing his hand, until you are seduced or he is rejected. It's all or nothing. In 2008, Rupert Murdoch, confounded by Boris' emergence and apparent loucheness, enumerated for me each of the above five points against Boris. But by 2012, Murdoch has become a keen Boris devotee. Smitten. Charmed."

Michael Wolff, *GQ*, February 5, 2013.

"Johnson's first year in charge of the capital has refuted the malicious forecasts of his foes and tentatively confirmed those of his fans.

London has not collapsed into a Billy Bunter comedy routine. The most incompetent central government of recent times, lauded by Johnson's enemies, has visited on London its most severe postwar crisis. The mayor has not panicked.

Johnson has changed the style and language of politics. His tendency to make every topic a joke, often at his own expense, was regarded as an engaging liability. It had appeal outside the charmed circle of political literates, but was predicted to have a short lifespan.

How could you have a mayor who said gosh, crumbs and crikey; who claimed to have 'played God at 10'; who wants a 'grand smashing of PlayStations'; and who professed to identify with the Incredible Hulk, since 'the madder Hulk gets, the stronger Hulk gets'?"

Simon Jenkins, the *Guardian*, April 30, 2009.